Tolerant Islam

vs.

Extremism

"Freedom is the essence and the central message of Islam. Anything that is not based on freedom but on ignorance and compulsion, is not Islam."

Tolerant Islam vs. Extremism
Maryam Rajavi

A selection of five speeches and an article

ISBN: 978-2-9554295-1-8

Published August 2016 by
National Council of Resistance of Iran
15, rue des Gords 95430 Auvers sur Oise- France

" There is no compulsion in religion."
-The Quran

" People are either your brothers in religion or your equals
in creation and humanity."
(Ali, companion of the Prophet)

Table of Contents

Introduction

Thirty-eight years after an authoritarian regime seized power in Iran under the banner of Islam, quarter of a century after the Persian Gulf war, 15 years after September 11, 2001 and the war in Afghanistan, 13 years after the US invasion of Iraq which opened its doors to the fundamentalists ruling Iran, and in the sixth year of Bashar Assad and the Iranian regime's bloodbath in Syria, there is hardly any place in the world that has remained away from the harms of Islamic fundamentalism and the terrorism emanating from it.

The terrorist attacks of January and November 2015 in Paris, December 2015 in California, March 2016 in Belgium, the explosion of a Russian airliner over the Sinai Peninsula in November 2015, the shooting rampage in Orlando, Florida, in June 2016 and the slaughter of innocent people in Nice in July 2016, clearly demonstrate that this evil phenomenon has not limited itself to Islamic countries.

No one can dispute the fact that the conflicts in the Middle East, and particularly the international community's failure to support the people of Syria against war crimes and crimes against humanity perpetrated by Bashar Assad, and its silence over the massacre of the people of Iraq at the hands of the Iranian regime and its puppet government in Baghdad, had a significant impact on the emergence, expansion and empowerment of the Islamic State (ISIS/ISIL or

Daesh). Just as no one can ignore the fundamentalists' taking advantage of some shortfalls in Muslim communities in Europe.

Some tend to conflate Islam and extremism, arguing that the present predicament basically emanates from the approach of Islam. They, thus, exonerate the Iranian regime and the governments of Maliki and Bashar Assad or minimize the significance of their roles.

There are also those who shrink the scope of this threat to one sect and highlight Sunni extremism as the main danger, forgetting other aspects of extremism operating under the banner of Islam so much that they propose seeking assistance from Shiite fundamentalists to conquer Sunni fundamentalists. Meanwhile, the convergence of behind-the-scenes interests has made matters even more complicated.

The purpose of this book is not to offer an exhaustive analysis of the phenomenon, but to shed light on and answer a natural question: What is the genuine outlook of Islam on these crimes? Do those who commit such atrocities really represent Islam? The answer is a resounding "no"!

Then, the next question would be: What is the position of Islam on key issues such as "popular sovereignty", "the principle of freedom" and "indiscriminate terrorism and violence"?

This manuscript is a compilation of excerpts from speeches and an article by the Iranian Resistance's President-elect Maryam Rajavi, a Muslim woman, who has led a relentless struggle to establish democracy, freedom and human rights in Iran.

She has consistently exposed and strongly denounced the mullahs' exploitation of Islam, and their regressive and fossilized ideology which benefits from the reactionary misinterpretation of the pure teachings of the Quran and the Prophet of Islam as a superficial school of thought that promotes suppression, misogyny and terrorism.

In contrast, she represents a voice that champions genuine

Islam which is democratic and tolerant.

It goes without saying that Maryam Rajavi's remarks were made in specific contexts at a particular time and place, and deal with prevailing issues and questions of their respective periods. Yet a feature of the content at hand, is that the underlying concepts and ideas are the products of a sweeping confrontation against a regime that is the source and inspiration of Islamic fundamentalism in today's world. In addition, these ideas have served and will continue to serve as the practical guidelines for an extensive and protracted struggle.

The concepts, traditions and pure values of Islam, cleansed of any imposed reactionary and exploitative disposition, have been turned into courses of action that manage collective relationships and construct a methodology for the overall struggle.

There Is No Compulsion in Religion

Excerpts of Maryam Rajavi's remarks at a conference entitled, "Democratic and Tolerant Islam against Fundamentalist, Religious Dictatorship"

Paris – July 3, 2015

Extensive portions of the Middle East are burning in the inferno of terrorism and war. It is the evil of fundamentalism that has established savagery and regression with a religious mask.

Today, I would like to underscore the fact that Islam opposes compulsion in religion or the imposition of any form of religion on citizens. Quite to the contrary, Islam emphasizes that freedom is indispensable to human society.

In today's Iran, the ruling mullahs have enchained our nation through incessant executions, torture, limb amputation, eye-gouging, and acid attacks on women as well as by causing rampant poverty.

Five days ago, the mullahs amputated the fingers of two young men in Mashhad. This horrific act of barbarity shocked the world, prompting Amnesty International to say that this ruthless and vicious punishment reflects the inhumane behavior of a state that rules through oppression.

This inhumane regime rests on the principle of *velayat-e faqih* (absolute clerical rule) and is the godfather of the likes of ISIS (Islamic State or Daesh) and Boko Haram.

All of these forces, regardless of their identity or the explicit claims they make, share a common inhumane ideology and underlying belief systems:

— Forceful imposition of religion;

— Establishment of absolute tyranny under the banner of the rule of God;

— Resorting to terrorism and expansionism under the pretext of exporting "revolution" and promoting "religion";

— Elimination, suppression and humiliation of women;

— And, trampling upon all human and divine principles in order to preserve their own rule.

Therefore, the notion of an Islamic Caliphate that today has cast a shadow over parts of Syria and Iraq is an incomplete miniature of a larger model established by Khomeini under the name of *velayat-e faqih* (absolute clerical rule) in Iran more than three decades ago.

Thirty years ago, Khomeini used to say, "People should be seared and branded in order to rectify society."[1]

And today the main motto of ISIS is, "Sharia law can never be enforced without the use of force."

An important weapon used by Islamic fundamentalists is *Takfir* (ex-communication) by which they target opponents of the reactionary Sharia.

But Khomeini was the founding father of the concept of *Takfir* in contemporary times. In 1988, he issued a *fatwa*

(religious decree) in his own handwriting in which he branded all prisoners belonging to the main opposition People's Mojahedin Organization of Iran (PMOI/MEK) as apostates and condemned them to mass execution. Subsequently, 30,000 political prisoners were massacred, including those affiliated with other opposition groups.

Therefore, first, in our times, the institution and promotion of fundamentalism and extremism under the guise of Islam, as a system of governance, came to fruition with the *velayat-e faqih* regime in Iran. Second, the fundamentalists' version of Islam is a religion of compulsion, stripping human beings of their free will, while the genuine Islam and the message of the Quran reject compulsory religion and any compulsion under the name of religion.

Freedom, the true essence of Islam

At this point, let us refer to the Quran, which introduces the true message of Islam.

— Has the Qur'an not said: There is no compulsion in religion?

— Isn't the message of Islam, compassion and emancipation?

— Do nearly all the chapters of the Quran not start with the phrase "in the name of God, the Most Compassionate, the Most Merciful"?

— Is Islam not the religion of tolerance and forgiveness?

— Did the Prophet Muhammed not forgive his enemies during the conquest of Mecca? And,

— Did he not present the charter of brotherhood and pluralism in Medina?

Indeed, freedom is the real essence of Islam.

So, what Iran's ruling mullahs and their ideological offspring, including the ISIS and Boko Haram, say runs counter to Islam and is utter blasphemy.

These verses are from the Quran:

"Debate with them in a way that is best."[2]

"Those who listen to speech and follow the best of it. Those are the ones Allah has guided, and those are people of wisdom."[3]

"Produce your proof, if you should be truthful."[4]

"Consult them in the matter."[5]

Indeed, the word of God neither coerces nor intimidates people. It rather encourages them to listen, reason, debate and consult with one another. These are what God Almighty decreed to Prophet Muhammed:

"You have come to provide guidance, not to watch over and control people."

"We sent you only to give people hope and advice."

"We sent you only as Mercy for all the people of the world."

The Holy Quran[6] has mandated the Prophet to be the harbinger of friendship and love among people, to unshackle their chains, and to promote tolerance and indulgence, all of which ensure that human society remains free and liberated.

From an anthropologic perspective, Islam and the Quran recognize that the most important attributes of human beings are freedom and the sense of responsibility that emanates from such an inherent volition. [7]

The Quran considers human beings as free and in control of their own destiny:

"Indeed, God will not change the condition of a people until they change what is in themselves." [8]

Islam promotes freedom of expression, and the security to challenge and criticize rulers. It does not prohibit people from doing so.

The Great Prophet repeatedly said, "No nation ever becomes clean and refined, unless the meek and the deprived can obtain their rights from those in power without fear and stutters."[9]

Similarly, throughout his reign, Imam Ali always defended

the rights of his opponents and critics.

Therefore, I say to my fellow compatriots and particularly the valiant youths of Iran:

Stand firm and resolute against the mullahs' impositions and precepts cloaked under the banner of Islam.

Lashing those who do not fast and suppressing women under the pretext of improper veiling have nothing to do with Islam. You must rise to resist this oppression.

Condemn the oppression and subjugation of our Sunni countrymen and other religious minorities because it represents a form of enmity against the entire Iranian nation.

Islam rejects anything that would undermine the freedom and free choice of human beings. It rejects compulsion in religion, in prayer and in veiling.

According to the Quran and traditions of the Prophet Muhammed, Islam is a dynamic ideology. Its edicts must be interpreted in the context of specific times or locations. The dynamism of the Quran, reflected in *Muhkamat* and *Motashabihat*, is one of the most distinctive characteristics of Islam.

Accordingly, two diametrically opposite versions of Islam are arrayed against one another: the Islam of freedom versus the religion of compulsion and coercion.

In the words of the Iranian Resistance Leader Massoud Rajavi: "One Islam advocates compassion, forgiveness and emancipation, while the other is sinister and ruthless. One is based on ignorance and compulsion, the other relies on freedom and free choice. One promotes darkness; the other is the standard bearer for liberty, unity and emancipation. The confrontation between these two versions of Islam is also a battle of destiny for the Iranian people and history, and represents one of the most important linchpins for the progress of modern humanity."[10]

With this mindset, Massoud Rajavi founded a democratic

movement, which opposed regression, a movement that emerged as the main barrier against religious fundamentalism. Today, this movement is a torch in the hands of the people of Iran and the nations of the region, representing the only beacon of hope for overcoming the monster of religious fascism and terrorism.

Shiite-Sunni fraternity

Islam rejects all forms of religious strife and hostility. It defends freedom, compassion and tolerance.

Today, the Iranian regime, its militias and other vicious extremist groups justify their crimes under the name of Islam. They portray their own power struggle as a Sunni-Shiite conflict.

For a long time, no such war existed in our region until Khomeini seized power in Iran. He sowed the seeds of discord and fratricide by continuing the war with Iraq, with the motto of "liberating Quds (Jerusalem) via Karbala", to expand his hegemony all over the region.

Inside Iran, he imposed dual oppression on the Sunnis by arresting and executing them and destroying their mosques, among other measures. On the eve of the holy month of Ramadan, the mullahs executed a political prisoner, who was a sports champion from Kurdistan.

In the past two years, a large number of Sunnis, including six Kurdish political prisoners, were executed in Gohardasht Prison, three Kurdish political prisoners were executed in Orumieh prison, and 34 Sunni Baluchi prisoners were executed in the cities of Chabahar, Zahedan and Zabol. The regime also assassinated Sunni clerics and citizens in Sistan-va-Baluchistan province.[11]

The same policy is carried out in the form of genocide of the Sunnis in Iraq and in the form of massacring innocent people in Syria.

In Iran, the mullahs have massacred the Shiite PMOI by the

thousands because they unmasked the mullahs' demagoguery. Similarly, they stop at nothing to conspire against the combatants of freedom in Camp Liberty, Iraq, including the continuing and criminal siege of the camp, and the dispatching of regime's Intelligence Ministry teams to the gates of Camp Liberty for a psychological warfare and to prepare the grounds for another human catastrophe.

Therefore, both Shiites and Sunnis have a common enemy: the fundamentalist theocracy ruling Iran.

Today, genuine Shiites are identified by their full-fledged enmity to the mullahs' regime in Iran and their belief that Sunnis are their brothers.

Imam Ali, the first Shiite Imam and the cousin of the Prophet, went even further than the issue of Shiites, Sunnis and believers in other faiths to say, "There are two types of people: Either your brethren in religion or those who are like you in creation."

Therefore, please allow me to tell the brother nations and all the people in the region that there can be an end to the carnage and conflict which the Iranian regime has fomented in your countries under the banner of Islam. The solution is to stand in solidarity with the Iranian Resistance and resist the Iranian regime and its accomplices, namely Bashar Assad and those groupings in Iraq, Yemen, Lebanon and Syria that are under the thumb of the Iranian regime.

So long as this regime is in power in Iran, the people of Iran and other nations in the Middle East will not enjoy freedom and democracy.

Therefore, the solution lies in the eviction of this regime from the entire region and in toppling the Caliph of regression and terrorism in Iran.[12]

Our positions and beliefs

As a Muslim woman, believing in separation of religion and state, and on behalf of a generation that has been defending the genuine Islam preached by Muhammed against fundamentalism and religious dictatorship for the past five decades, I declare:

We reject compulsory religion and any form of compulsion in religion.

Despotism under the name of Islam, the medieval Sharia laws, and the excommunication of opponents whether Shiite or Sunni, are against Islam and the liberating message of Muhammed.

In our view, the essence of Islam is freedom; freedom from all forms of compulsion, oppression and exploitation.

We follow the genuine Islam, the tolerant and democratic Islam, which defends popular sovereignty and gender equality.

We reject religious discrimination and defend the rights of followers of other religions and faiths.

Our Islam believes in brotherhood among all religions.

Sectarian wars and sowing discord among Shiites and Sunnis are the sinister products of the fundamentalist regime in Iran, which seeks to prolong its anti-Islamic and inhumane Caliphate.

Indeed, our God is the God of freedom, our Muhammed is the Prophet of compassion and emancipation, and our Islam is a religion that respects freedom of choice.

Freedom, the Glow of God

Everyone asks what does Islam say about freedom?
Is Islam a motivating force for freedom or an obstacle to it?

International Islamic-Arab Conference in Solidarity with
the Iranian Resistance and Ashraf
Paris – August 4, 2012 (Ramadan)

Our Prophet Muhammed (PBUH) had a very simple and short message: Say there is no God but the Almighty and attain prosperity and be free.

It is the same message that calls on everyone today to say: Dictators are doomed to go.

Say that the religious fascism in Iran will fail.

Say that the manifestations of tyranny and exploitation will crumble and you will attain prosperity.

This is why that in every call to prayer at dawn or sunset during the month of Ramadan, and in the phrase "there is no God but Allah," we hear echoes about freedom. It delivers the message of rejecting idols that encourage enslavement and servitude; it promises the downfall of *velayat-e faqih* (absolute clerical rule) and the birth of a free, stable and just society.

A reminder about the Iranian Revolution

Thirty-three years ago, the people of Iran rose for freedom but instead they found themselves facing a tyranny under the guise of religion...

Khomeini started to crack down on basic freedoms. He turned Iran's spring of freedom into a bloodbath. Every oppressive measure was justified under the name of Islam. Khomeini's abuse of Islam to justify his oppression and tyranny was his worst betrayal of Islam. Iranians in their thousands have fallen victim to the regime's crimes committed both in prisons and on the frontlines of the (Iran-Iraq) war. But Khomeini's and the mullahs' greater crime and betrayal was that they committed all these atrocities in the name of Islam. Through their words and deeds, they introduced Islam to the world as a tool in the hands of the most vicious dictatorship that suppresses freedoms.

Today, everyone from the Islamic and Arab world to Iran is seeking freedom. All nations demand freedom and reject dictatorships.

Everyone asks what Islam says about freedom? Is Islam a motivating force for freedom or is it an obstacle to it?

How does the conduct of Khomeini, his heirs and other fundamentalists who gained power after Khomeini in many parts of the Islamic world, relate to Islam?

I want to tell you about our own experience in Iran and about the confrontation of the Muslim PMOI with a regime that calls itself Islamic. The passage of time has only intensified this confrontation.

Today, more than three decades have passed and the Muslim PMOI, i.e. whose members are in camps Ashraf and Liberty, continues to remain the main opposition to the regime.

Indeed, what does a Muslim and Iranian organization like the PMOI say about Islam? What has been their position with respect to Khomeini from the outset?

The meaning of creation

Freedom is the meaning and ultimate goal of Creation. Since its creation, the trajectory of existence in the universe has moved away from blind obligation, compulsion and coercion to freedom. Islam and the Quran are committed to the same spirit and goal.

So, when we speak about freedom, equality, justice and rejection of exploitation in Islam, it is based on the profound essence and philosophy of Creation. This is what has been described in the Quran as *Ketab-e Mubin* (or the Book of Revelation).

Freedom embodies divine trust in human nature. The purpose of piety is to lift this inherent freedom to the highest point possible.

Striving towards progress and perfection for both an individual and society is tantamount to becoming freer and more liberated. How? By setting aside all restrictive elements, shattering blind fate and overcoming self-alienation, whether it relates to a person, nature or society at large. This is the true meaning of salvation. This is the meaning of piety and the true prosperity that human beings can obtain.

So, how can we possibly reconcile Islam with tyranny and suppression of freedoms?

The fact is that there is no ideology or school of thought in the world that is more distant and more alien to genuine Islam and more irreconcilable with it than Islamic fundamentalism.

Our religion was brought by a prophet whom God describes as one who came to destroy the chains and unshackle the masses of people.

«وَيَضَعُ عَنْهُمْ إِصْرَهُمْ وَالأَغْلاَلَ الَّتِي كَانَتْ عَلَيْهِمْ»

"He releases them from their heavy burdens and from the yokes that are upon them."[13]

Unshackling chains from people's hands and feet means freedom from compulsion and coercion, freedom from repression, freedom from any form of oppression and exploitation, and freedom of human beings in benefitting from the product of their own labor.

In fact, this is the most significant distinction between genuine Islam and the fundamentalist interpretation of Islam.

On the one hand, there is an Islam that defends oppression, aggression and exploitation, and on the other hand there is another Islam that opposes exploitation and tyranny.

Yes, Islam is a religion that cherishes the freedom of human beings. Islam has never wanted human beings to be captives or doomed to suppression and exploitation. On the contrary, it sees humankind as God's heir on Earth to the extent that the angels (i.e. the forces of nature turning the wheels of evolution) bow to human beings.

«وَإِذْ قُلْنَا لِلْمَلَائِكَةِ اسْجُدُواْ لآدَمَ فَسَجَدُواْ»

And behold, We said to the angels: "Bow down to Adam" and they bowed down.[14]

Consciousness and free will

In monotheistic anthropology, humankind is recognized by consciousness and freedom. He or she has free will and the right to freedom and free choice. The notion of the Day of Judgment clearly attests to the responsibility and accountability of man for his deeds and therefore reflects his freedom and free will.

The Quran emphasizes that it is the human being himself/herself who has the capacity to choose their fate.

«إِنَّا هَدَيْنَاهُ السَّبِيلَ إِمَّا شَاكِرًا وَإِمَّا كَفُورًا»

"We showed him the Way: whether he be grateful or

ungrateful [rests on his will]."[15]

Human beings are capable of distinguishing between good and evil.

«فَأَلْهَمَهَا فُجُورَهَا وَ تَقْوِيهَا»

"So He reveals to it its way of evil and its way of good. And it is Man himself who can change his own destiny."[16]

«إِنَّ اللَّهَ لاَ يُغَيِّرُ مَا بِقَوْمٍ حَتَّى يُغَيِّرُواْ مَا بِأَنْفُسِهِمْ»

"Allah does not improve a people's lot unless they change what is in their hearts."[17]

This is why no one should worship anyone but The Almighty God and should not consider an equal to Him.

«وَلاَ نُشْرِكَ بِهِ شَيْئًا وَلاَ يَتَّخِذَ بَعْضُنَا بَعْضاً أَرْبَابًا مِّن دُونِ اللَّهِ»

"That we worship no other but Allah; that we associate no partners with him; that we erect not, from among ourselves, Lords and patrons other than Allah."[18]

There is no compulsion in religion

Freedom is the essence and the message of Islam. Therefore, whatever that is not based on freedom and is instead fed from compulsion, coercion and ignorance cannot be defined as Islam.

We say that believing in and practicing Islam must be based on one's free will, free choice, awareness and freedom, not on compulsion.

No religion can be imposed upon people, because faith is something that is in one's heart and his conviction. Everyone is free to choose his/her religion. There is a verse in the Quran that says: «لا إكراه في الدين»

Let there be no compulsion in religion.[19]

In verse 20 of The Jonah, God tells the Prophet Muhammed:

«وَلَوْ شَاء رَبُّكَ لآمَنَ مَن فِي الأَرْضِ كُلُّهُمْ جَمِيعًا أَفَأَنتَ تُكْرِهُ النَّاسَ حَتَّى يَكُونُواْ مُؤْمِنِينَ»

"If it had been thy Lord's will, they would all have believed,- all who are on earth! wilt thou then compel mankind, against their will, to believe!"[20]

Let's turn to The Prophet Hud, verse 28, where Noah tells his people:

«قَالَ يَا قَوْمِ أَرَأَيْتُمْ إِن كُنتُ عَلَى بَيِّنَةٍ مِّن رَّبِّيَ وَآتَانِي رَحْمَةً مِّنْ عِندِهِ فَعُمِّيَتْ عَلَيْكُمْ أَنُلْزِمُكُمُوهَا وَأَنتُمْ لَهَا كَارِهُونَ»

"O my people! See ye if [it be that] I have a Clear Sign from my Lord, and that He hath sent Mercy unto me from His own presence, but that the Mercy hath been obscured from your sight? Shall we compel you to accept it when ye are averse to it?"[21]

Indeed, monotheism and Islam are intertwined with freedom of humankind and their right to free choice. Anything that is against freedom is rejected by Islam.

No to compulsory religion, no to compulsory worship, no to compulsory veil.

Islam is a religion of latitude and autonomy, which respects human beings and honors their essence more than anything else.

As it has been mentioned in the famous letter of Imam Ali, the Prophet's cousin and son-in-law and the Fourth Caliph of Muslims, to Malik Ashtar, the Governor of Egypt.

«أَشْعِرْ قَلْبَكَ الرَّحْمَةَ لِلرَّعِيَّه وَ الْمَحَبَّةَ لَهُمْ وَ اللُّطْفَ بِهِمْ وَ لَا تَكُونَنَّ عَلَيْهِمْ سَبُعاً ضَارِياً تَغْتَنِمُ أَكْلَهُمْ فَإِنَّهُمْ صِنْفَان إِمَّا أَخٌ لَكَ فِي الدِّينِ وَ إِمَّا نَظِيرٌ لَكَ فِي الْخَلْقِ»

"Open your heart to the people and be kind to them. Beware of being brutal to them, because people are either your brothers in religion or like you in creation and humanity…"[22]

On this basis, the Quran says there is no distinctions among prophets. Therefore, we consider Jesus as our messenger and we do not separate the path of Moses from that of Muhammed.

Defending the rights of opponents

Islam also espouses freedom of expression and encourages - not forbids - people to criticize and oppose their rulers. Islamic pioneers even held debates with agnostics and atheists, respecting their right to freedom of expression.

When the Prophet conquered Mecca, he granted clemency to his most spiteful opponents. Let us read from The Cattle which advises the true followers of Islam "not to curse at those who worship things other than God."

The tradition of Imam Ali in dealing with his opponents is also very telling. The most vehement opponents of Imam Ali in those days were the *Kharajites*. They openly cursed Imam Ali (PBUH), so much so that his companions sought to arrest them. Ali, however, forbid them from doing so and even granted his opponents a share from the Muslims' common treasury. He also did not accuse those who rose up to fight him of "heresy" or "hypocrisy."

In the treaty of Malik Ashtar, the Governor of Egypt at the time, we read the following on freedom of criticism. Imam Ali says, "The closest aides to you must be those who criticize you more and praise you less... Spend some of your time with those in need and allow them to attend a public meeting. Treat them humbly and forbid guards and soldiers to suppress fearless expression of opinion....

"I heard the Prophet repeatedly saying that no nation could ever be pure and dignified if the weak were unable to obtain their rights from those in power without fear, worry or hesitation."[23]

Yes, this is the entire story. Let people speak out without fear or worry. Let the oppressed express what they have in their hearts. Let the deprived and the enchained speak out.

Two contradictory "Islams"

Islam inspires the Iranian Resistance's perseverance against the most brutal dictatorship of our time. It is based on freedom. Therefore, two opposite and contradictory "Islams" have lined up against each other in Iran's contemporary history.

On the one side is a deceitful and reactionary Islam that advocates tyranny, despotism and exploitation.

On the other side is the Islam of truthfulness, honesty, compassion, emancipation and an Islam whose message is freedom.

In diametric opposition to the reactionary principle of *velayat-e faqih* (the absolute rule of the clergy), we advocate a democratic Islam that recognizes popular sovereignty as the people's chief right.

In contrast to the warmongering and export of terrorism and fundamentalism under the banner of Islam, we follow an Islam that advocates peace, friendship and brotherhood among nations.

In contrast to the ruling mullahs' misogyny, we advocate an Islam that considers women's equality as its cause. This Islam relies on the equality and emancipation of women. 1,000 pioneering women in Ashraf and Liberty are the most vivid examples of this conviction.[24]

In the face of discrimination and religious despotism, we have risen to defend the principle of freedom of religion.

In contrast to the mullahs' Sharia law that relies on the rulings issued 1,400 years ago, we believe in the dynamism and evolution of the Quran and Islam.

The Iranian Resistance is proud that it could rescue the true spirit of Islam and its exalted culture from the darkness of retrogression, that it could introduce the humanitarian and emancipating message of Islam and distinguish it from totalitarianism, fanaticism and discrimination through the movement's suffering and sacrifice and its democratic and tolerant outlook on Islam.

The Iranian Resistance has been able to draw a clear distinction between the genuine message of Islam and reactionary interpretations of it.

Islam Advocates Popular Sovereignty

*Conference entitled, "Islam against dictatorship and
fundamentalism, promoting popular sovereignty"
Paris – September 4, 2010*

I t is part of the Mercy of Allah that thou dost deal gently with them Wert thou severe or harsh-hearted, they would have broken away from about thee: so pass over [Their faults], and ask for [Allah's] forgiveness for them; and consult them in affairs [of moment]. Then, when thou hast taken a decision put thy trust in Allah. For Allah loves those who put their trust [in Him]."25

Distinguished Guests,
Brothers and Sisters,
I wish that your prayers, fasting and heartfelt worship would be accepted by God Almighty.

Ramadan is the month of *Taqva* (restraint), the month of elevating our human essence, the month of getting our hearts closer together, the month of fraternity, for which today's societies long.

From the perspective of genuine Islam, Ramadan is the month of emancipation for which Prophet Muhammed was given his mandate: to remove the shackles gripping mankind.[26]

On this momentous and blessed occasion, your presence here provides me with a unique opportunity to speak on behalf of millions of my compatriots in Iran, who rose up against the regime last summer; to speak about the massive oppression which the mullahs' brutal regime has imposed on my people and my religion under the banner of the *velayat-e faqih* (absolute clerical rule).

I should also highlight the main essence and spirit of the *velayat-e faqih*, which rests on the usurpation of popular sovereignty. I would also want to show that in the context of genuine Islam, sovereignty is the most important right belonging to the people.

I hope this short presentation would echo the freedom cries of millions of Iranians who last summer were chanting the very meaningful slogan of "down with the principle of the *velayat-e faqih*."

This slogan inspires the continuation of the uprising and is the rallying cry of a people who, owing to the scale of the current repression, have joined voices in nightly protests on rooftops to condemn the crackdown on the uprisings as well as the execution of political prisoners.

Why has the slogan of "down with the principle of the *velayat-e faqih*" inspired the uprisings in Iran?

Velayat-e faqih is the source and the pillar of a 30-year dark oppression, manifested in daily suppression, torture and the killing of the most enlightened and selfless children of the Iranian nation, especially the most faithful Muslim and Mojahed men and women.

During the grand gathering of Iranians in Taverny,[27] I heard my brother Sid Ahmad Ghozali addressing leaders of Arab and Muslim countries and saying, "Beware that no regime in the world has killed so many Muslims and in the most brutal manner."

Indeed, *velayat-e faqih* means unbridled dictatorship, which charges the children of the Iranian nation with *Moharebeh* (waging war on God) and sentences them to death merely for participating in demonstrations, reading the publications of the People's Mojahedin Organization of Iran (PMOI/MEK) or meeting their relatives in Camp Ashraf, Iraq. This dictatorship rapes and murders those arrested during the uprising in the secret Kahrizak detention center.

Why has the slogan of "down with the principle of the *velayat-e faqih*" inspired the uprisings in Iran?

Because when Khomeini returned to Iran (in 1979), his first and foremost betrayal of the people of Iran and the country's revolutionaries was carried out under the banner of *velayat-e faqih*.

While he was in Paris, Khomeini used to say that he was a "student of theology" and would merely "return to the city of Qom and let those qualified to run the affairs of the country." In practice, however, he not only monopolized power but discarded the newly-drafted constitution for the country; he refused to convene the legislative and constituent assembly, which he had officially promised to set up. Instead, he imposed the *velayat-e faqih* constitution through the Assembly of Experts that was comprised of his handpicked clerics.

The PMOI, as the largest organized Muslim organization, formally declared that it would not vote for the Constitution because of its opposition to the principle of *velayat-e faqih*. The PMOI asserted that in their view sovereignty belonged to the people and their vote.

Khomeini saw this as the PMOI's greatest sin and to this date it continues to remain the main cause for their suppression and murder.

Today, after such a painful and catastrophic experience, my discourse will not be limited to rejecting a false and unfounded unorthodoxy.

I want also to emphasize that for the Iranian people and those who rose up, *velayat-e faqih* means the three-decade totalitarianism of Khomeini and Khamenei.

The world saw that during the uprising, the Iranian people, students and young people set fire to and stomped on pictures of Khomeini and Khamenei in Tehran University and elsewhere.

Indeed, *velayat-e faqih* means an extensive and dark oppressive rule which has squandered my homeland's vast natural resources through war, suppression, and destructive policies.

It has forced the flight of Iran's scientists and scholars. Over 80 percent of the population, which sits atop vast oil reserves, has been forced to live below the poverty line. Many of them are forced to sell their kidneys to make ends meet, or to pay their children's expenses and rent.

Velayat-e faqih means ruthless state-sponsored terrorism that issues *fatwa*s in the 21st century for the secret chain murders of writers, intellectuals and honorable and innocent priests, such as Bishop Hovespian-Mehr, with impunity.

Velayat-e faqih means issuing *fatwa*s for genocide and the massacre of 30,000 political prisoners, many of whom had finished serving their terms and were waiting to be released. Upon Khomeini's written and extrajudicial decree, they were hanged in prisons of Tehran and other Iranian cities in 1988. Khamenei and all present leaders and officials of the regime were involved in this mass murder and continue to refuse disclosing exactly how many they killed.

Velayat-e faqih means exporting fundamentalism and engulfing countries in the Middle East in the quagmire of terrorism and bloodshed. *Velayat-e faqih* means the ominous program to build nuclear weapons.

Indeed, *velayat-e faqih* means a cunning demagoguery, which has shed all this blood, perpetrated all this corruption under the name of religion, and tarnished the image of Islam.

Is Islam not the religion of mercy and emancipation? Does the Quran not say about Prophet Muhammed that "We sent thee not, but as a Mercy for all creatures?"[28]

And do the chapters of the Holy Quran not begin with the phrase "In the name of God, the Most Merciful and Most Compassionate?" Are Islam and the Quran not based on the act of "consultation in the affairs?" And is Islam not the religion of tolerance and forgiveness?

Truly, can one find any conscientious human being or caring and faithful Muslim not aggrieved over so much injustice to and distortion of Islam and the Quran, and who would not cry out to expose these demagogues and liars?

Velayat-e Faqih

The principle of the *velayat-e faqih*, which is an isolated school of thought even among Shiite and Sunni scholars, was first invoked by Khomeini. He promoted this doctrine during his religious sermons in Najaf, Iraq, in the 1960s and published it in a book entitled, "The Government of Islam." In this book, Khomeini tries to give priority to the rulings of the cleric-supported Sharia (which was based on a deviated interpretation of Islam and filled with misogyny, religious discrimination and concepts that violate human rights) to prove the need for exclusive governance by the mullahs. Khomeini also revealed in this book the despotic and medieval nature of the regime he had in mind and described it as akin to a guardian of minors.[29]

Khomeini's superficial arguments in this book in defense of *velayat-e faqih* is not a doctrine based on solid religious contentions but rather sought to prepare the so-called theoretical underpinnings for seizing political power. These were not ideas that he had suddenly discovered at the time of the book's publication at the age of 70.[30]

Before the theocracy assumed power in Iran in 1979, the near unanimous majority of Shiite scholars opposed the idea of *velayat-e faqih*. After Khomeini took power, however, some began to follow and promote his theory.

If we were to loosely translate *velayat* into governance, this theory opines that governance is an inalienable right that God has bestowed upon the clergy.

Although this theory contradicts the true spirit of Islam and the traditions of the Prophet and leaders of Islam, in order to present a definition of *velayat-e faqih* we can review over three decades of a dark rule under the same name in Iran and find a vivid practical meaning:

- *Velayat-e faqih* is based on monopolizing power in the hands of the "supreme leader." Therefore, it is not comparable to any other theocracy. According to the regime's constitution and laws, all government agencies, including the Legislature, the Executive, the Judiciary, the Armed Forces, the secret and intelligence services, the Police, and the largest economic foundations, as well as the political and ideological control of universities and all ministries, government offices, military, disciplinary and judicial organizations are placed under the authority of the *vali-e faqih* (supreme leader) and he is exempt from accountability to anyone. Khomeini, however, was not satisfied with that and said, "What is enshrined in the Constitution is only part of the authorities of the *velayat-e faqih* and not all of it."[31]

Later, when the Constitution was amended, they changed the title of the *velayat-e faqih* to the Absolute *Velayat-e faqih* (absolute rule of the jurisprudent).[32]

As one of the theoreticians of the velayat-e faqih, Ahmad Azari Qomi, wrote in 1988, "*Velayat-e faqih* means absolute religious and legal guardianship of the people by the *faqih*. This guardianship applies to the entire world and that which exists in it, whether earthbound or flying creatures, inanimate objects, plants, animals, and anything in any way related to collective or individual human life, all human affairs, and their belongings and assets. It also covers God's religion from the primary and second commandments to prayers, politics, society, family life, obligations, from *mostahabat* and execrable, to permissible and unlawful."[33]

The *faqih* "can prevent daily prayers, fasting, pilgrimage, promoting virtue and prohibiting vice if he deems appropriate, temporarily and under his rule and or in such circumstances destroy the house of a believer and divorce his wife."[34]

The *velayat-e faqih* regime does not accord the slightest legitimacy to people's suffrage and these peddlers of religion see themselves as God's vice-regent on Earth and pretend to gain their legitimacy from Divine Revelation.

And the current Supreme Leader Ali Khamenei is famous for saying, "What right do the majority of people have to sign the Constitution and make it binding?"[35]

For the *velayat-e faqih* regime, the highest value and the most sacrosanct principle is remaining in power. For this reason, they see themselves to be permitted to trample upon all humanitarian, legal, national and international principles and to perpetrate all kinds of heinous crimes and atrocities or to engage in deception.

Khomeini personally justified the violation of all principles, traditions and pledges. In a 1988 letter to the then-President, Khamenei, Khomeini wrote, "The *vali-e faqih* is empowered to abrogate the religious commitments he has undertaken to the people should he find them contrary to the interests of the nation and Islam. Governing is one dimension of the absolute authority of the *velayat-e faqih* and takes precedence over all secondary commandments, even prayer, fasting and the Hajj pilgrimage."[36]

The entire essence of *velayat-e faqih* can be clearly seen in the above quotes.

Before seizing power, Khomeini argued that the need for *velayat-e faqih* is to implement reactionary Sharia laws. After seizing power, however, he proved that it was only a quest for power, for which he violated all moral, humanitarian and religious principles.

Khomeini's explicit remarks in this regard have been documented in the collections of his speeches when he said that in order to protect Islam (i.e. his own rule), lying is an obligation, drinking alcohol is an obligation, and spying is an obligation.[37]

The clerical regime's endless evil over the past three decades has taken place with the same unchanged interpretation of *velayat-e faqih*: The eight-year war with Iraq with one million killed on the Iranian side, the massacre of 30,000 political prisoners upon a hand-written edict by Khomeini, systematic rape of female political prisoners, hostage-taking and bombing of the House of God in Mecca, usurping of Iran's wealth and revenues, astronomical fraud in the elections and tides of deception and lies.

As can be seen, the dispute is not over Islam or its rituals, the permissible or the unlawful; the main focus is simply on an insane obsession with power.

The Quran says, "There is the type of man whose speech about this world's life may dazzle thee, and he calls Allah to witness about what is in his heart; yet he is the most contentious of enemies. When he turns his back, his aim everywhere is to spread mischief through the earth and destroy crops and cattle."[38]

Islam and popular sovereignty

Islam recognizes the right to sovereignty as an inalienable and the highest right for the people. Islam also profoundly respects the rights which emanate from popular sovereignty.

The Quran states unequivocally that God appointed human beings as his own image on Earth. As it is stated in the Quran, God breathed His spirit into human beings,[39] meaning that they became Godlike and his vicegerent on Earth. In Chapter Narration, it is stated, "And We wished to be Gracious to those who were being depressed in the land, to make them leaders and make them heirs."[40]

How can one invoke the ignorant and corrupt rule of the *velayat-e faqih* from this noble philosophy?

There is an eternal message in the notion of Muhammed (PBUH) being the last of the prophets. The message is that social progress has reached a point where people themselves can assume their role as guides and leaders in the framework of the world outlook and principles which Islam and the Quran have offered. The notion clearly contradicts all the lies that Khomeini and likeminded individuals in other branches of Islam are staking a claim to by invoking the *velayat-e faqih* or Islamic rule, including guardianship over all peoples, whether minors or adults.

In essence, the people's sovereignty has at its core the concepts of freedom and equality and this is the main theme and the true message of genuine Islam.

The question of human freedom is the main question that distinguishes between democratic Islam and a fundamentalist interpretation of it.

From the point of view of Islam, consciousness and freedom constitute the unique attributes of human beings, who are able to make choices. This is why human beings are responsible for what they do and must account for their actions in the afterlife. Without enjoying freedom, how can one explain man's responsibility? And why must he account for it in another world?

From the point of view of Islam, all human beings, regardless of race, gender or nationality, are equal. The most fundamental value revolves around the human character and the laudable actions that it inspires. As noted in the Chapter entitled "Apartments," the Quran does not recognize as predominant values the differences with respect to gender, race or nationality. It says the highest value is *Taqva* (piety or self-restraint).

Prophet Muhammed personally proclaimed the principle of "equality among all human beings". Mecca was conquered while it was a hotbed of enemies of the Prophet. In a short speech to his former enemies, the Prophet said: Know that all people are children of Adam, and Adam was born from the soil.

In his famous sermon, known as *Hajj-ul-wida* (the final pilgrimage), the Prophet said, "In Islam, people are equal. They are equal like a two pan balance. All of them come from Adam and Eve. No man has primacy over the other; Arabs or non-Arabs have no predominance over one another, except for their virtue and self-restraint."[41]

As for the equality of men and women, it should be noted that there is no gender discrimination in the Quran. It sees women and men equally fit for leading the society. In the Chapter Repentance, it is said, "The Believers, men and women, are not separate and are protectors of one another." (Repentance, verse 71)

In the Family of Imran, the Quran says, "Women and men are made from the same body and their efforts have the same value."[42]

In Islam, equality also means the denial of religious discrimination. Religious discrimination is a pillar of fundamentalism. But in Islam, any discrimination against followers of other religions is rejected.

In The Cow, verse 136, the Quran addresses all believers in Islam and says, "Say ye: 'We believe in Allah, Abraham, Isma'il, Isaac, Jacob, and the Tribes, and that given to Moses and Jesus, and that given to [all] prophets from their Lord: We make no difference between one and another of them: And we bow to Allah [in Islam].' "

Therefore, in diametric opposition to *velayat-e faqih* as a system defending exploitation and inequality, Islam emphasizes the foundations for popular sovereignty which are freedom, equality, and rejection of all forms of religious and gender discrimination.

Popular sovereignty is one of the inalienable rights in Islam. It is a right that cannot be violated, and it is not limited or conditional. True Muslims believe that God's will is basically and historically manifested in the social sphere through the sovereignty of the people.

Freedom of choice and suffrage

Islam is a religion where every human being's right to free choice is respected. The choices and votes of all human beings are profoundly respected in Islam.

From the point of view of Islam and the Quran, consciousness and freedom constitute the unique attributes of human beings. Man is not doomed to a certain fate and is able to break out of any coercion. The Quran says that God ordered the angels to bow before humans, meaning that human beings have the capability to conquer the forces of nature.

In numerous verses in the Quran, man's right to freedom of choice has been underlined.

In the early days of Islam, Prophet Muhammed repeatedly provided the opportunity for all the people to directly express their views and to vote directly. To this end, he invoked the tradition of *Bei'at* (statement of allegiance) when making important decisions or signing major pacts. The most famous of these are the *Bei'at* of women, *Bei'at* of Rezvan and *Bei'at* of Al-Ghadir. While different from the present-day elections which have become prevalent in the past couple of centuries, *Bei'at* was a popular tradition in the specific political and social contexts of 14 centuries ago.

Despite his affinity to the Prophet of Islam and his pristine understanding of Islam as well as his personal qualifications to lead the society of his own era, on which all followers of the Prophet agreed, Imam Ali accepted the leadership 35 years after *Hijra* only when, as he put it, the population was insisting on it for a full week. Absent that public outcry, Imam Ali was not prepared to assume the leadership.

Pluralism

Believing in the principle of popular sovereignty is therefore a requisite to pluralism, tolerance, and respect for the opinions and faith of others.

There is no precedence - and there can be none - in genuine Islam for all powers being consolidated in the hands of a single clergyman, or for the imposition of beliefs, religion or the government of "dissolution in the *velayat-e faqih*" on other people.

Islam advocates freedom of thought, as well as religious and political tolerance. The Quran's guidance in this regard is:

"Those who eschew Evil,- and fall not into its worship,- and turn to Allah [in repentance],- for them is Good News: so announce the

Good News to My Servants,- Those who listen to the Word, and follow the best [meaning] in it: those are the ones whom Allah has guided, and those are the ones endued with understanding."[43]

The Prophet of Islam believed that the diversity of opinions, ideas and thoughts was a source of prosperity and he famously said, "Differences (of opinion) among my nation is the cause of prosperity."

Imam Ali, the first Shiite Imam, says that one of the objectives behind the coming of prophets was to extract the treasures in the minds of human beings. The task of the *velayat-e faqih*, on the other hand, is to denigrate human beings and destroy the treasure in their minds.

Another important example of the Prophet's Traditions on the freedom of thoughts and religion, was his famous treaty with the Jews residing in Medina. Equal rights, as well as respect for the blood, family, dignity and properties of both sides were recognized in this treaty, and underlined repeatedly. There were no differences in this charter between the rights of Jews and those of Muslims, while their respective tribes' internal autonomy was accepted. In addition, both Jews and Muslims were free in practicing their own rituals and religious duties and no party was allowed to violate the rights of the other.[44]

Iran's great historian and researcher, the late Abdol-Hossein Zarrinkoob, considered tolerance as "the mother of Islamic civilization" and wrote, "Islam replaced the old world's prejudices and zealotry with a spirit of tolerance and cooperation... Islam intervened when the spirit of tolerance and moderation was dying... Islam breathed a new spirit into a world which had been captivated by religious and ethnic zeal... Islam advised that believers in the holy books should tolerate one another and sign treaties, and be interested in science and life..."

Islamic Civilization began to crumble only when ethnic and local zeal destroyed their unity and tolerance. Such tolerance towards the adherents to the Book – who were known among Muslims as *Ahl-e Zemmeh* (those having obligations) and *Mo'ahed* (the allies) -- was based on some kind of peaceful co-existence which was unknown to the Europe of the Middle Ages.

In fact, despite the restrictions the *Ahl-e Zemmeh* faced in *Dar-ol Islam* (under the government of Islam), Islam guaranteed their freedoms and comfort as much as possible. Rarely were there any instances where the *Ahl-e Zemmeh* were prosecuted without breaching their obligations. The Prophet recommended friendship and tolerance towards them. There is a story narrated from the Prophet who said any one who oppresses a *Mo'ahed* (an ally), or imposes on him more than what he affords to do, I will judge the former on Resurrection Day…

As for the heathens, Islam was not as harsh as other religions of those days. Despite theoretical differences over the nature of faith, practically only a verbal testimony was often accepted as the criterion for believing in Islam. Even the Prophet showed tolerance and leniency towards the hypocrites whom he knew.

Altogether, the history of Islam and Muslims confirms the judgment of historian Joseph Arthur de Gobineas [(1816-1882) former French Ambassador to Iran], about Muslim's sublimity and excellence, who said, if religious conviction is separated from political necessity, there is no religion more tolerant and less prejudiced than Islam.[45]

Legislation by the people

To justify their savage rule and give preference to the mullahs' Sharia laws, the mullahs deceptively argue that people do not deserve to draft the laws they need for proper social, economic and political relations; they argue that it is the *vali-e faqih* (who is supposedly connected to the source of Revelation) who can form the basis for all relations in society.

During the Constitutional Revolution (1906), Sheikh Fadhlollah

Nouri, who was Khomeini's ideological father, declared it as being "against Islam and unlawful" to write and draft the Constitution. He argued that drafting a constitution would be akin to drafting laws against the laws of Islam, compelling people to follow laws that have not been devised by the Islamic Sharia.

Seventy years later, when Khomeini took power, he could not oppose legislation of laws because of the progressive state of society at the time and evolution of the Iranian people's freedom movement. However, to bring the process of legislation under his control, he initially set up a reactionary parliament all of whose members were required to sign "heartfelt allegiance to the *velayat-e faqih*." Secondly, he put the reins of the parliament in the hands of six clergies appointed by himself, called the Council of Guardians, to veto any law ratified by the parliament that contradicts the mullahs' Sharia. In this way, no law can be passed in the parliament unless it is within the framework of beliefs and interests of the *velayat-e faqih*.

The mullahs justify this tyrannical process by exploiting Islam. One of the *velayat-e faqih* theoreticians, Mullah Mohammad Taghi Mesbah Yazdi, said in this regard, "Originally, the right to legislation belongs to the Almighty God who is omnipotent and most knowledgeable. Mankind is not entitled to the right of writing laws because he does not have enough knowledge about his own affairs. Therefore, Islam and the Quran have been handed down to man as the most holistic law for a desirable life so that he can learn the path toward a good life... Any rule and any law that adapts to the absolute will ruling the universe and humanity, that is the will of God, is considered legitimate, even if it is not accepted by the government or the people. On the contrary, any rule and any law that does not comply with the Divine will is not considered legitimate, even if the government and the people accept it... And the acceptance of any law, except the Divine Law, is considered paganism the same way that obeying and worshipping anything but God is considered paganism. Of course, it is possible that God grants permission to the prophets, the imams, or their representatives and heirs to make laws or devise codes of practice."[46]

The laws which the fundamentalists impose on people's social and political life under the banner of Islam and make them mandatory have no relevance to Islam whatsoever. In a limited number of issues, the Quran has put forth a number of edicts, which have to be seen in their specific historical context. Given that historical context, these edicts were a leap forward at the time and paved the way for a progressive set of relationships.

The Quran has essentially dealt with the interpretation of the world, the evolutionary process, the emancipating essence of historical development and the responsibility of human beings to attain freedom, equality and build a society in which human values have the highest priority. Nevertheless, the determination of social, economic and political arrangements is left to the people themselves, who should undertake this task while inspired by those very values but consistent with each historical epoch.

The edicts fundamentalists impose on people as Islamic laws are riddled with inequality, misogyny, religious discrimination and human rights abuses and are in no way related to Islam. Neither stoning to death nor limb amputation nor raping female and male prisoners have anything to do with Islam and the Quran.

On this basis, we ruled out the mullahs' viewpoints, laws, and heinous conduct which were forcibly imposed on people under the pretext of protecting Islam and its prayers and rituals.

I must emphasize that anything that ignores people's free and voluntary choice is not Islamic.

Rejection of compulsion and coercion is not only essential to the selection of a religion, but is also true for Muslims in carrying out their prayers and other rituals. Religious affairs, including one's method of worship, comply with religious principles only when they are carried out on the basis of a Muslim's free will and choice.

Dynamism of the Quran

The *velayat-e faqih* regime justifies its rule with the intention of implementing the Sharia laws. At best, they are rigid edicts, which the mullahs, ignorant of the dynamism of the Quran and Islam, intend to implement exactly as they were 14 centuries ago.

As far as the social and economic edicts are concerned, Islam and the Quran do not claim that there are fixed edicts that carry weight forever. The Quran emphasizes that social and economic edicts must be designed in such a way that the dying and counter-evolutionary forces would not find the possibility of obstructing the progress and advancement of humanity.

In The Family of Imran, verse 7, the Quran explicitly says that its verses are of two types: *Muhkam* (basic or fundamental) and *Muteshabeh* (allegorical). Fundamental verses are essentially those that form the convictional foundations of Islam. They contain the philosophical, ontological, and anthropological content and bases of Islam.

The allegorical verses, however, basically deal with daily lifestyle and edicts. They are not fixed or constant and they can be adapted or tailored, on the basis of a monotheistic theology, to a specific period in history in the context of the particular level of progress in human society.

The Iranian Resistance's Leader Massoud Rajavi describes this quality as "the secret to the endurance and vitality of the Quran and Islam."

In a speech on the dynamism of the Quran and Islam, he said, "In its interpretation of Islam, the PMOI believes that the first quality of Islam is its dynamism. Islam is not a fixed and rigid Sharia. If this is a religion belonging to centuries ago, why should we adhere to it? The reactionary clergy have made a business out of jurisprudence (i.e. to adapt religious precepts to the circumstances in their own era), and still, they sanction stoning and public floggings? Actually, the mullahs present their own crimes to the world under the name of Islam while the ultimate goal of creating such a social and political atmosphere is common knowledge.

"Ironically, one wonders if what the mullahs present is really Islam, then what is reactionary ideology and barbarism? How should one describe barbarity and cruelty? Let us challenge them by demanding just one example from the epoch of Imam Ali or the Prophet where they did the same things (as the mullahs), because stoning has never been an Islamic punishment...

"Furthermore, how is it that the mullahs take advantage of the latest technological, scientific, and professional achievements of the 20th century, but their punishments and retributions are in the style of thousands of years ago? We challenge the mullahs to explain why they pursue mid-range and long-range missiles, nuclear, biological and chemical weapons and do not use the wheels, horses and mangonels of the Dark Ages? Why do they, on the one hand, take advantage of the latest technical advances of the capitalist era at the expense of the Iranian people, while on the other hand they follow the punitive laws of thousands of years ago such as stoning and limb amputations? Why do they throw people off a cliff (as a form of punishment)? Which one are we to believe?

"Let us use a better example for this. Any sincere person understands that a coast is the destination or the goal for a sailing ship. In our discussion, the goal or our destination is unity or oneness. By this, we do not mean individualism, but social unity and a society devoid of discrimination. Allegorical edicts are the adaptations made in special circumstances at a specific time. This adaptation is not opportunistic but motivated, evolutionary, creative and active.

"Back to our example. Allegorical edicts concern the style of rowing, adjustment of direction and the pace of the ship based on the circumstances for which the ship's captain makes decisions. This is what fundamental and allegorical edicts mean. The fundamental edicts are the ones that tell you of the strategy, and the allegorical edicts are the tactics that help implement that strategy... They are the tools, instruments, applications and practical guidelines to reach the goal. They set the limits.

"Obviously, if we refrain from scholastic arguments and are neither dogmatic nor irresponsible in interpreting the edicts, we can understand that genuine instruments and applications guarantee achievement of the goal and protection of its authenticity. The same is true for genuine goals that need their own authentic tools. In other words, in the context of a concrete and objective approach, we cannot ignore or underestimate the tools and instruments and at the same time we have to ensure that they serve the goal. They should not contradict, oppose or obstruct it."[47]

The faith of consultation

By respecting the sovereignty of the people, Islam rejects all forms of despotism and totalitarianism.

In The Family of Imran, verse 159, the Prophet is told, "It is part of the Mercy of Allah that thou dost deal gently with them Wert thou severe or harsh-hearted, they would have broken away from about thee: so pass over [Their faults], and ask for [Allah's] forgiveness for them; and consult them in affairs [of moment]."[48]

This verse was sent down after the Prophet suffered a setback in the War of Ohod. The defeat was the consequence of a plan that the Prophet's companions had insisted on. Nevertheless, God orders the Prophet to consult with them even after the setback. In fact, by emphasizing "consultation," the Quran points everyone towards an exalted value.

There is a chapter in the Quran called, "Consultation," where the capacity for consultation is underlined as one of the most noble qualities of human beings.

The chapter reads in part: "Those who hearken to their Lord, and establish regular Prayer; who [conduct] their affairs by mutual Consultation; who spend out of what We bestow on them for Sustenance." (verse 38)

In this verse, the value of consulting with others is set equal to daily prayers and charity to others.[49]

By emphasizing on this value, the Prophet of Islam never made important decisions without consulting others, although he received Divine Revelation. There were even cases where the Prophet put others' views before his own. There is a famous saying from the Prophet Muhammed: "Consultation is a tradition of the Prophet and despotism is an evil characteristic of human beings."[50]

In his last speech known as the Farewell Pilgrimage (*Hajj-ul-Wida*), the Prophet warned Muslims against being misled. He said despotism is a telltale sign of deviation.

The opinions of progressive clergy

In the decades and centuries past, many scholars of Islam, who refused to put their religion at the service of the ruling regimes, have underscored these facts. Contrary to those who were trying to present religious justification for the oppressive monarchic dictatorship, Ayatollah Mirza Hussein Na'ini, one of the greatest Shiite Marjas (source of emulation) in the early 20th Century wrote a book in 1909 on the need to establish a constitutional form of government and rejected a despotic form of governance. With rational argumentations and by citing the verses of the Quran and the sayings of the Prophet as well as the discourse in Shiite jurisprudence, he demonstrated that

- Islam rejects despotic rule;
- Islam respects freedom and equality;
- A government based on law and parliament is the most viable form of government.

In his book, Ayatollah Na'ini decisively condemned dictatorship under the cloak of religion and wrote, "Despotic Ulema are usurpers of religion and deceive the abased. Unseating the wretched roots of political and governmental dictatorship is far easier than uprooting religious tyranny."[51]

In the midst of the Constitutional movement, the most prominent source of imitation for Shiites, Khorassani, gave unlimited support to the movement. Along with Sheikh Mazandarani and Haj Mirza Khalil Tehrani, he reiterated in an edict, "In the absence of the 12th Imam, it is a religious necessity that the government be run by the republic of the people."[52]

We remember when Khomeini was establishing his dictatorship, Ayatollah Seyyed Mahmoud Taleqani, the most popular cleric who defended the goals of the anti-monarchic revolution, said in one of his speeches: "Compulsion under the banner of religion is the most dangerous kind of compulsion; that is to shackle people under the name of God with what is not from God. Preventing them from protesting and criticizing. Banning freedom of activities... This is while Islam invites all to mercy and freedom... and Imam Ali said: All tyrants are doomed to eradication..."

Confronting Khomeini, Taleqani cried out: "Live your own lives. Let the people undertake their own responsibility... Set aside despotism under the banner of religion."[53]

By insisting on such genuine convictions, the Resistance movement has been able to defeat Khomeini's fundamentalism and Islam in the social and cultural realms. This is why the PMOI has been the main target of suppression throughout the past three decades.

Democratic Islam: Example of the People's Mojahedin

Conference entitled, "Arabic-Islamic Solidarity with Ashraf"
Paris – August 13, 2011

There have been many books, research documents and speeches about freedom and popular sovereignty and about the fact that Islam is a religion that respects freedom, with the spirit of all its teachings and instructions culminating in the emancipation of mankind. Such writings and speeches and every theoretical and intellectual effort in this regard is of course invaluable. However, this notion can find new richness and depth and be proven only when it turns into the cornerstone of a social struggle. In other words, only if it is concretely manifested and materialized in a freedom-loving movement, or a certain set of social relationships.

Particularly when the mullahs rule in Iran and Islam is introduced as a religion based on tyranny, it is all the more necessary to demonstrate a concrete and definite experience that shows the liberating spirit and message of Islam in practice.

It is exactly at this point where the significance of the People's Mojahedin Organization of Iran (PMOI/MEK), their endurance and perseverance for nearly half a century and their continued commitment to genuine Islam all become evident.

The PMOI movement demonstrated its deep conviction in democratic Islam by making tremendous sacrifices in the course of an arduous and long struggle.

The PMOI entered into the political and social scene in 1965, relying on a genuine and democratic interpretation of Islam.

The movement's number one priority has been to challenge the reactionary and deviant manipulation and interpretation of Islam and the Quran. It fought against the kind of manipulation which made Islam subordinate to suppressive rulers.

It opposed the type of misappropriation that sought to show that Islam defended the status quo and justified discrimination, injustice and exploitation of human beings by other human beings.

The founders of the PMOI established their movement with a remarkable message: the principal dispute, they said, is not between believers in God and non-believers, but between the oppressed and the oppressors. This message targeted the pillars of Khomeini's fundamentalist view of Islam.

Since 40 years ago, Massoud Rajavi, the Iranian Resistance's Leader, has led a theoretical, cultural and ideological campaign against fundamentalism.

Part of this struggle was carried out in the Shah's prisons. And an important part of it was accomplished during the complex domestic and international circumstances in 1978 and 1979 when Khomeini emerged as an undisputed religious and political leader.

Rajavi continued to lead this movement after the religious dictatorship was established in Iran, defining the ideological and practical foundations of the struggle.

He showed that genuine Islam, more than any other religion,

defends equality, justice, freedom, and emancipation; that it has the greatest capacity to reject discrimination, exploitation and despotism and establish a democratic society.

In the 1970s and in the Shah's prisons, the PMOI readily turned down a decree signed by senior clerics affiliated with Khomeini, which excommunicated atheists and Marxists. They defied that edict, which would have set a fundamental precedent for religious suppression and discrimination.

In 1975, the PMOI was shattered in the course of an internal coup. But instead of seeking retribution and succumbing to ideological and religious confrontations, the PMOI laid emphasis on the main danger in Islamic fundamentalism, which threatened all the people of Iran.

Upon seizing power, Khomeini called his reactionary government the "Islamic Revolution." Our movement, however, never accepted to refer to the regime as "Islamic" or to refer to what had taken place as an "Islamic Revolution." On the contrary, in the midst of Khomeini's social and religious popularity, our Resistance accepted all the risks and de-facto political damages and drew a firm line between the two camps. This is why Khomeini branded the PMOI as "hypocrites" and, using this label, massacred 30,000 PMOI men and women in prisons.

Over the past three decades, however, the PMOI – armed with a democratic and tolerant Islam -- has defeated the religious dictatorship in the cultural and ideological realms and destroyed the pillars of the regime's Islamic legitimacy among the Iranian nation. Citing the Quran, history of Islam and symbols of Shiism, they have revealed the mullahs' deception to the people of Iran. They have proven that Islam does not contradict democracy and pluralism. On the contrary, genuine Islam is summed up in the freedom of mankind from all kinds of shackles.

The PMOI's dispute with Khomeini was over one word: freedom. This dispute has continued to this day.

In his first and last meeting with Khomeini, Massoud Rajavi told him about freedoms. He based his argument on the Quran and on Imam Ali's letter to Malik Ashtar. In that meeting, Khomeini was forced to say, "Islam is attentive to freedom more than anything else ..." And the newspapers ran this statement as a headline in those days...

Indeed, Khomeini and the mullahs' regime see the PMOI as their worst enemy because they are staunch advocates of freedom.

Massoud Rajavi's only sin was that he rejected Khomeini's religious dictatorship under the name of *velayat-e faqih* and loudly denounced it as being against Islam and its liberating teachings.

Massoud Rajavi did not accept Khomeini's invitation to replace people's sovereignty and suffrage with Khomeini's Sofiani (tyrannical) *velayat-e faqih*.

He said: When it comes to the country's affairs, it is not right to draw boundaries between Muslims and non-Muslims and discriminate against them. In a word, the PMOI argued against Khomeini, saying that sovereignty belongs to the people not to the mullahs. Freedom of parties and freedom of expression are the rights of dissidents and Islam protects these rights.

In those days, when Khomeini launched a wave of misogyny and sent his thugs to the streets to attack women with the motto of "either the veil or a hit on the head", the PMOI formally denounced compulsory veiling and the regime's repressive approach while the PMOI women who wore scarves themselves actually defended unveiled women against the fundamentalists' onslaught.

In 1979, there was a debate over the country's Constitution just as debates now occur in countries affected by the Arab Spring. We did not vote for the Constitution of the *velayat-e faqih* because it took away people's sovereignty from them, and because *velayat-e faqih* is against the Muhammedan Islam and against the Prophet's traditions more than anything else, trampling over the rights of the people. Such flagrant opposition incited a tide of crackdown and

killings against our movement.

In 1981, when Khomeini wanted to have the Retribution Bill (implementing the draconian punishments of *Qisas*) passed in the mullahs' parliament, the PMOI called it anti-Islamic and "an inhumane bill."

In the same years, the Khomeini regime sentenced to execution the leader of the group that had shattered the PMOI under the Shah and who had killed and burned the bodies of some of the movement's leaders. The PMOI, however, urged the regime to grant them amnesty, a move that provoked astonishment.

The PMOI said they were inspired by the Prophet Muhammed's clemency who forgave his sworn enemies after the conquest of Mecca. Khomeini, of course, did not heed this request and executed him.

Our movement also opposed Khomeini's policy of export of the "revolution," which he pursued from the onset as an Islamic platform. The PMOI declared this policy as being against the peace-seeking spirit of Islam and against the interests of the people of Iran. This is why the PMOI hoisted the flag of peace during Khomeini's eight-year war with Iraq, and in the midst of his hysteric warmongering. The PMOI was not bedazzled by Khomeini's demagoguery who presented his belligerence under the name of Islam. We showed that peace is not only a political obligation but one of the fundamental principles of democratic Islam.

In 1985, women stepped into leadership positions within the Iranian Resistance. In the eyes of the mullahs, this was an unforgivable heresy. For the oppressed women of Iran, however, it was a leap towards the future and a powerful motivation for seeking freedom and equality.

Islam has the greatest respect for mankind and especially for women. It calls for women's equality and freedom. One of the most brilliant facets of the Prophet's mission was emancipating and respecting women.

The Iranian Resistance's pioneering women, who have undertaken the most crucial responsibilities in a liberation movement, have been inspired by democratic Islam and by Islam's conviction in equality. The ten-year endurance and steadfastness in Camp Ashraf, Iraq, which presents one of the greatest and most astonishing examples of resistance movements in our time, was led by these women.

In 1985, in the midst of the mullahs' religious hysteria, the PMOI movement enunciated the concept of the separation of religion and state. This was an incredible initiative on the part of a Muslim force and, indeed, could not have been serious or impactful unless a Muslim force took the initiative. Through this initiative, the PMOI drew a boundary between genuine Islam and the fundamentalist outlook. They showed that genuine Islam defended religious freedom and rejected totalitarian rule and religious tyranny.

As Massoud Rajavi has said, "In diametric opposition to Khomeini, the Islam we believe in does not need to prove its truth through coercion. We are deeply convinced that Islam can blossom only in the absence of all discriminations, privileges, and when there is no political or social coercion."

In 1988, Khomeini massacred 30,000 of our prisoners. At the same time, the PMOI released thousands of prisoners of war they had taken from Khomeini and showed that their understanding of democratic Islam is the very forgiveness and mercy which the Prophet has promulgated.

The reverence of Islam is in its message of compassion, which is respect for human rights, a message of clemency and generosity, and finally respect for individual and social freedoms.

Indeed, we follow an Islam which, in the words of the Quran, views the life of one human as having the same value and importance as the existence of all humanity." And if any one saved a life, it would be as if he saved the life of the whole people."[54]

As the Iranian Resistance has repeatedly declared, "When Iran is free from the mullahs' oppression, we will call for an end to the death penalty and elimination of all forms of cruel punishments and we are committed to this."

Contrary to the *velayat-e faqih*'s insane greed for power in the name of religion, we follow in the footsteps of the Prophet (PBUH), who the Quran described as "a reminder of God Almighty and not someone who exercises supremacy over the people."[55]

In the midst of the anti-monarchic revolution, Khomeini sent a message to the PMOI through various means, including by his son Ahmad. The message was that if the PMOI would accept *velayat-e faqih* and the leadership of "the *Imam*" (Khomeini), all doors to entering government and taking government positions would be open for them. Given the extensive popularity and credibility the PMOI had gained through years of struggle against the Shah while they were an organization that believed in Islam, Khomeini knew full well that the PMOI could be one of the greatest assets for him. The PMOI's answer to Khomeini, however, terribly upset him.

They said they were willing to cooperate with him only if the common criterion and basis for the two sides would be free elections and the popular vote. But Khomeini did not accept and instead undertook a policy of repression, murder and tyranny. It was thus proven how just and necessary it was to draw a firm line of opposition to Khomeini.

In 2009, in the course of the Iranian people's uprisings to overthrow the *velayat-e faqih* regime, our Resistance defended the rights, security and protection of leaders of the regime's defeated faction who displayed some support for the uprisings for a brief period of time. The PMOI repeatedly condemned all forms of oppression and suppression that the *velayat-e faqih* would use against them. This while the same leaders were involved in the massacre of the PMOI for many years.

The Islam in which we believe does not teach rivalry, greed for power or pursuing narrow group interests, but it rather teaches us forgiveness, leniency and commitment to the ideal of freedom of an enchained nation.

Between our movement's self-interest and attainting power on the one hand, and remaining committed to the ideal of freedom and democracy and earning the trust of our compatriots on the other, we have chosen the latter.

It is our mission to sacrifice ourselves so that the Iranian people can have the ability to choose freely.

This is why I have reiterated time and again:

The goal of this movement has never been and is not to gain power at any cost. Our goal is to guarantee freedom and democracy at any cost.

Our cause is freedom, equality and our people's right to suffrage. Our goal is to establish a republic based on the separation of religion and state where all religions enjoy equal rights. Our platform is summarized in three words: Freedom, democracy and equality.

And finally, the PMOI has demonstrated its commitment to Muhammedan Islam and the Islam of compassion and freedom, in raising a generation of dedicated and faithful men and women who have displayed astonishing perseverance in Ashraf and have pioneered the struggle for freedom. "Those who fulfil the covenant of Allah and fail not in their plighted word." [56]

And those who put the broader interests of other human beings above their own, although they might be very much in need themselves; "but give them preference over themselves, even though poverty was their [own lot]."[57]

They have found Islam in their practical commitment to honesty and making sacrifice. Honesty in its Quranic meaning where the honest are placed higher than the martyrs. And making sacrifices not only by sacrificing their lives but also by sacrificing their loved ones and their properties. They have proven and presented Islam in their practice: in their pure humane relationships, in humbleness and avoiding selfishness, in their affability, generosity, beneficence, love and dedication to the cause of others.

They have hoisted the banner of Muhammedan Islam in their struggle for equality of men and women on the basis of the verse "Verily the most honored of you in the sight of Allah is

[he who is] the most righteous of you."[58] They reject all forms of discrimination and inequality among human beings and have rebelled against oppressive discrimination among men and women.

Mercy for All

*Gathering of French, Arab and Iranian personalities on the
anniversary of the birth of the Prophet Muhammed
Paris – April 2006*

Honorable Sisters and Brothers,
Dear Friends,
Felicitations on the birth of Muhammed (PBUH),
the Prophet of Islam. I would like to use this opportunity to
also congratulate the Christians of the world and particularly my
Christian compatriots on the Easter.

Muslims the world over celebrate the auspicious birth of the
Love of God, Prophet Muhammed.

Muhammed was an orphan child and a shepherd starting at a
young age. This underprivileged young man, however, ended up
transforming the world and opening the doors to a world of unity,
mercy and tolerance for humankind.

When we glance over his life and personality, we discover that
a great injustice has been done to him and his message. We learn
that fundamentalists such as the mullahs ruling Iran, those who
advocate terrorism and misogyny, are not his followers, but his
worst enemies.

Since the beginning in Mecca, Muhammed was known for being trustworthy (*amin*), which meant that he was a righteous man.

Muhammed's humane characteristics caught the eye of Khadijah, who was an exceptional and independent woman and a merchant in Mecca, and she asked him to marry her. The Prophet accepted although Khadijah was much older than him. This great woman became Muhammed's friend, companion and supporter until the end of her life. In difficult times and under tremendous pressure after the Prophet began his mission, she defended him with all her power and love.

Nonetheless, the great watershed moment in the life of Muhammed that opened a new path for mankind was when he was chosen as a prophet. But how could he create a civilized society by rallying a people who lived in ignorance?

He realized this goal with his message of unity, fraternity, mercy and tolerance. He thus injected humanity into that world.

Muhammed succeeded in having a new culture prevail in primitive societies at the time, who previously routinely buried infant girls.

One the most brilliant facets of the Prophet's mission was the emancipation of women. When his daughter Fatimah entered the room, Muhammed always stood up as a sign of respect, and laid down his robe on the floor so she could sit on it.

The Prophet's treatment of his daughter was so different from the prevailing culture in those days that many criticized him for it. One day, when an Arab man was describing to the Prophet how he had buried his infant daughter alive before he became a Muslim, Muhammed began to cry and denounced this practice, saying: "He who does not have mercy and emotion will not receive the mercy of God."

He behaved in such a way that no one felt uncomfortable or afraid when expressing their views in front of him. He welcomed and implemented people's right opinions or suggestions, even if he disagreed with them personally.

Muhammed's love and affection was endless and unilateral. He did not discriminate between young and old. Despite his great status, he greeted children when passing through the streets. There were many instances when he would join in their games and spend time with them. Children would gather around him wherever they would see him.

Even a moment of interaction with the Prophet was enough to provoke admiration. People were in awe of his candor and empathy, and so began to believe in him and his message.

The scope of his clemency and mercy was immense. Even in the War of Ohod, when his enemies killed his uncle, Hamzah, and a number of his other companions, he repeatedly prayed, "Oh, God! Forgive this tribe for hurting me, because they are ignorant!"

Muhammed (PBUH) said: I have not come for damnation. I have been chosen to spread "mercy."

He also said: "Everyone's neighbor is like himself. No one should speak ill to or mistreat his neighbor."

There is also another famous saying from him: Be kind to the residents on Earth and have mercy on them so that the God of Heavens would have mercy on you.

With his message of mercy and compassion, Muhammed conquered everyone's hearts and brought about major changes:

He conveyed the message of monotheism to people which was the harbinger for equality and brotherhood among all nations.

He said slaves are equal to free men and women.

He led the steadfast endurance of believers when they were banished to the *She'eb* of Abi-Talib and were placed under a blockade.

The people of Medina had been waging wars against one another for 100 years. He reconciled their differences and created peace and unity among them.

He created a pluralist society in Medina and drafted a charter for them according to which everyone in this society, whether Muslim or Jewish, was an equal member. They were free in observing their religious rituals and duties.

At a time when the lives of prisoners were worthless, the Prophet established the tradition of pardoning and releasing prisoners of war.

Women were allowed to take on the most significant social roles. They were granted rights to inheritance, property, and testimony, and all forms of insults and sexual accusations against them were forbidden.

Muhammed abrogated all misogynous traditions such as killing infant girls and the sex trade. He granted women the right to freely choose their husbands. Women's rights during marriage and their respect and security after divorce were recognized. Women were granted equal right to divorce. He also abrogated oppressive divorce methods by men.

He educated people about the equality of men and women and let women participate in the struggle and in social affairs.

He established a new social and economic order. He declared that all human beings are equal and rejected all racial and national privileges.

He set up progressive principles like the principle of presumption of innocence, which the world community relies upon even today.

He denounced earning money and gathering wealth through illicit methods, and chided some people's refusal to help the poor.

He advocated consultations and debate.

He obliged people to live together in peace with believers of other faiths and religions.

He taught believers to see their differences as an act of mercy. He replaced barbaric prejudice with a spirit of tolerance.

Yes, the image of Muhammed is not what the fundamentalist mullahs ruling Tehran depict. They have upended the message

of Muhammed and by attributing their own regressive thoughts and inhuman behavior to Islam, they have distorted its image...

So, we detest the message of terror and murder that Iran's ruling mullahs promote in the world under the banner of Islam. The massacre of political prisoners, the hanging of young people, the suppression of and discrimination against women, forcing women into prostitution, usurping of people's properties and the country's wealth, and terrorism are all but examples of actions being committed under the mullahs' rule in Iran. How can one make a connection between these actions and the Prophet's message of love, equality, brotherhood and tolerance?

Muhammed's message was peace. What does that have to do with the mullahs' bid to acquire nuclear weapons and pose a threat to the world?

As Muslims following in the footsteps of Muhammed, we have risen up against the religious dictatorship in Iran and see it as the worst enemy of the Prophet.

By following the Prophet's path, who embodied Mercy for

both worlds, we have risen to build a society based on freedom, tolerance and brotherhood.

We have learned from him to be kind to all people from every race, religion and nationality, love them and express solidarity with them.

And we seek his help to succeed in this struggle to put an end to tyranny.

The Truth of Islam

By Maryam Rajavi - July 2016

The crises of terrorism and tyranny under the name of Islam continue to confront both the Muslim and global communities as never before. The brutal killings of July 14 in Nice, July 4 in Medina, June 12 in Orlando and March 22 in Brussels confirmed the persistence of the threat that befell France, Brussels, Denmark, the U.S. and the rest of the world.

Viewing these attacks in their real context, which also includes the ongoing conflicts in the Middle East, will afford us more profound results: These incidents are the deliberate outcomes of a frightening and aggressive world outlook that tramples upon divine values on the pretext of defending religion. It attempts to put a veil of religious legitimacy on actions that by all accounts constitute murder. And, it portrays these actions as carrying the highest values by revering methods employed during the darkest periods of humanity.

Those who subscribe to this outlook consider themselves to be Muslims, acting as if they are the elite followers of a legitimate faith while all others, including the rest of Muslims, are complete heretics, worthy of either total domination or annihilation.

Steeped in this outlook, they allude to Quranic verses and the traditions of the Prophet of Islam, in a vain attempt to justify their actions. They masquerade as Islam an ideology that is summed up in tyranny, violence, sacrilege, inequality and misogyny. Is this really Islam or a complete perversion of it?

Coercion or freedom?

Since the outset when Prophet Mohammad invited all to accept a single God, he told people that this would bring them salvation. God said in the Holy Quran that the prophet had come to open the chains from people's hands and feet.

Prior to this, Jesus had said: Love one another just as the Lord loves you.

Before him, Moses invited people to a religion that considers human beings as part of one family, describing the various peoples, ethnicities, and tribes as branches that lead back to a single source.

So, all of us, as the children of Abraham, are brothers and sisters. What is essential in relations among human beings is not retribution, tyranny and exploitation, but freedom, compassion and unity.

For a long period of time, of course, oppressive rulers and forces interpreted Quranic verses in accordance with the most reactionary schools of thought. They attached many fabricated veneers to Islam. But the true message of Islam has survived.

In the course of this conflict, two diametrically opposed versions of Islam have emerged to confront one another:

One interpretation is based on tyranny while the other Islam rests on freedom.

The first promotes compulsion and deception, while the other relies on free and conscious choice. The first looks to the past and defends laws and social relationships of the past millennia, and the other defends universal human rights and underscores freedom. The first is based on a mechanical and fundamentalist reading, while the second is based on a dynamic reading tied to the explicit sayings of the Quran and the liberating spirit of Islam.

In order to justify religious compulsion and coercion, fundamentalists claim that when choosing Islam as a faith, the scope of freedoms are limited, and after accepting Islam each Muslim must submit to the coercive measures that the fundamentalists advocate. This is while every specific action and ritual in Islam is only valid when it springs from the individual's choice and volition. Islam teaches every follower to strive to engage in *Ijtihad*[9] (adapting general laws to the contemporaneous social setting).

Islamic fundamentalists consider the initial measures of Islam, which were in the direction of abolition of oppression, violence and inequality, as permanent and fixed commandments. After 1,400 years, they insist that humanity must remain stuck in that same historical spot.

This is while Islam opened a path on which humanity could take other steps in order to realize divine compassion and true human freedom.

At a time when women were not only deprived of owning property but had absolutely no economic rights, Islam, as a first step, recognized the rights of women to own property and declared that they deserve an inheritance at least half that of men. This decree heralded an age for the abolition of inequality. The intention of it was not that women will have only half the rights of men for all eternity.

In an age of barbarity, where one tribe carried out a wholesale slaughter of another over a single murder, the monotheistic religions instituted «*qisas*» (retribution) as a punishment commensurate with the scope of the crime committed. This opened a path for limiting punishments and respecting the lives of families and tribes to which the accused belonged. It was not an order to unleash ruthlessness.

In the age of slavery, Islam said that many sins can be forgiven through the freeing of slaves. This was a clear course-setting measure for the gradual abolition of slavery, and nothing less.

Besides, why do the fundamentalists who ignore the true direction or course-setting actions of the Quran and still rely on its verses, continue to ignore the Quran 's explicit sayings?

In The Family of Imran, verse 7, the Quran clearly says that some verses in the holy book are *Muhkamat* (foundational and not subject to change) while others are *Muteshabihat* (allegorical). However, it says, «Then those in whose hearts is perversity follow the part of it which is allegorical, seeking to mislead, and seeking to give it (their own) interpretation.»

Muhkamat are verses relating to foundational and non-changing principles such as the oneness of God, the Day of Judgment, equality among human beings, and personal responsibility.

Muteshabihat, on the other hand, are primarily related to social and economic regulations and edicts, as well as the methods and strategies to realize humanitarian and social values. These methods are predicated on historical and geographical circumstances, always changing and evolving in proportion to the advancements and progress made in particular epochs. What is important is that 1,400 years ago, these edicts and methods were far more advanced than the methods, traditions and standards prevalent in even the most advanced societies of that age, especially in the Arabian Peninsula that saw the advent of Islam. These laws heralded a vast economic and social transformation in that historical context.

The Quran has gone even further when it comes to recognizing the changing nature of socioeconomic laws and methods. The Quran was revealed to the Prophet of Islam over the course of a 23-year period. Many of the orders revealed in the early years of Islam that were proportional to the level of progress and advancement in the Muslim community ultimately changed during the final years of revelations and the Prophet's life. In The Cow, we read: «Whatever message We abrogate or cause to be forgotten, We bring one better than it or one like it. Knowest thou not that Allah is Possessor of power over all things?»[60]

The Bees talks about orders that replace others.[61] The first leader of Shiites, Imam Ali, states that the Quran says, «Some affairs were mandatory in their own times, but were annulled at a later point.»[62]

Despite all this, fundamentalists have expropriated the Quran, committing many crimes by falsely quoting Quranic verses based on a rudimentary understanding of the holy text to advance particular political agendas while referring to views that have been fabricated through the ages.

In addition to the rulings mentioned in the Quran, other rulings, the bulk of which are the mullahs' sharia, did not exist either during the life of the Prophet of Islam or in later years. They have rather been formulated by clerics in subsequent centuries.

Now that we know the Quran itself recognizes the termination of certain things and highlights the need to replace the old with the new, why should the rulings of clerics who lived a thousand years ago remain unchangeable? Why should Muslims not be able to critique these rulings and formulate laws and regulations that are proportional to the progress of society? Why should they follow rulings, many of which defend oppression and inequality, and are thereby un-Islamic? Truly, without a dynamic understanding of the Quran, any interpretation will inevitably be a perversion and must be firmly rejected.

The common beliefs of fundamentalists

All fundamentalists, from the mullahs ruling in Tehran, who are the ideological godfathers of Daesh (ISIS), to the militias affiliated with the Islamic Revolutionary Guards Corps' Qods Force in Iraq, or the Lebanese Hezbollah, Boko Haram, and Daesh, speak of Islam, but in reality they stand against the truth of Islam.

All of them - with their different names and faces - have a common belief summed up in their commitment to the reactionary Sharia and extremist implementation of it. This Sharia emerges in various forms, including religious coercion, tyrannical rule, misogyny, heresy, and rejection of moral and Islamic principles.

Coercive religion

When Khomeini and his clerical clique instituted their regime by suppressing those who had brought about the 1979 revolution, they imposed their reactionary ideology by chanting the slogan «Only One Party, the Party of God.» They suppressed women by chanting «either the veil or a hit on the head.» They then proceeded to force people to comply with the rules of a coercive religion through executions, torture and intimidation.

Three decades later, when Daesh began to appear on the scene, its main slogan was «Islamic Sharia will never be implemented without a weapon.» This is while anything that is accompanied by force and compulsion is diametrically opposed to the spirit of religion, and as the Quran has itself said: «There is no compulsion in religion.»

And the rituals that are mandatory for the followers of Islam, including daily prayers and fasting, are not considered valid unless they are purposeful (to get closer to God) or voluntary.

The establishment of despotic rule

Fundamentalists seek to establish a barbaric tyranny under the banner of Islam, referring to it with various names like the velayat-e faqih in Iran (absolute clerical rule), or the Islamic State or Caliphate. They claim that since they have risen up to implement Islamic laws, they are justified in using force and eliminating freedoms. But, tyranny is a contradiction of Islam. In the Quran, God tells his Prophet: «So remind. Thou art only one to remind.

Thou art not a warder over them —.» [63]

Two very important documents assist us to an extent in revealing Islam's true view regarding the behavior of rulers towards their people.

First is the letter written by Umar, the second Islamic Caliph

(586-644), to the people of Jerusalem in 636 after Muslims won a portion of the Byzantine Empire. In the letter, Umar wrote: «This is a promise of security that Umar, the leader of Muslims, is giving to the people of Jerusalem. I hereby guarantee the security of all residents, healthy or sick, including people's lives, property, churches, and crosses. I will not occupy or destroy their churches. Churches themselves or anything in their vicinity, crosses and properties will not be touched. No one will be able to force them to leave their land or abandon their faith. No one will be hurt. ... Anyone who leaves Jerusalem will be guaranteed safety for their lives and property until they reach a secure destination. And anyone who remains in the city will be safe.»[64]

The second is a letter from Ali bin Abitaleb, the Prophet's son-in-law, the fourth Caliph and the first leader of Shiites (518-661), who wrote to Malik Ashtar, after appointing him as the ruler of Egypt: «Harbor compassion, good behavior, and goodness towards people. You shall never act like a rabid animal towards them thinking that devouring them is fine. There are two kinds of people: those who are your brothers in faith, and those who are humans like you in creation. ... The best minister in your view should be a minister who tells you the bitter truth instead of admiring you for the words and deeds which the Lord does not accept for his friends. Improvement in the lives of the citizens must weigh more heavily in your thinking than taxing them, because taxes will not become available unless with development. So, if those who pay taxes complain about it being too heavy, give them discounts to the extent that they see improvement in their lives. Prevent your military forces from confronting the ordinary people so that their spokesperson can speak up without stuttering and without fear and concern. I have heard many times from the Prophet that no nation ever becomes clean and refined, unless the meek and the deprived can obtain their rights from those in power without stuttering, fear and concern.»[65]

Terrorism and the insane craving for power under the banner of «Jihad»

What today's fundamentalists introduce as «Jihad» or «Jihadism» is in reality nothing other than sheer terrorism and brutality. The meaning of jihad in the Quran is to rise up against injustice, something that has even been enshrined in the Universal Declaration of Human Rights. The Quran gives permission for jihad only to those who face injustices, are being murdered or forcibly exiled from their country.[66] This means that the Quran recognizes their right to stand up against injustice. In this context, what does such a struggle have to do with the seeking of domination by the mullahs over Syria, Iraq, Lebanon, or Yemen, or with the attempts by Daesh to dominate more territory and gain access to more oil fields?

In their minds, Muslims who oppose the rule of clerics or caliphs, as well as non-Muslims who refuse to surrender to them, are the primary targets of this so-called jihad.

Why do those who claim they declare jihad against the enemies of God live in peace and solidarity with Bashar Assad and Khamenei, while at the same time spraying unarmed people in concert halls or train stations with bullets?

Is it considered jihad when the mullahs ruling Iran unleash their armies in Syria to massacre hundreds of thousands of Syrian women, men and children while displacing over half the country's population?

Rejection of borders

Another common element among fundamentalists is the rejection of national borders and efforts to occupy other countries' territories. Today, Daesh has occupied portions of Iraq and Syria under the banner of an Islamic State while calling for the occupation of other countries. But the phrase «Islamic State» was something that was mentioned over three decades ago by Khomeini in his will. He demanded the creation of «an Islamic State with free and independent republics.» In the current constitution of the Iranian regime, the government is responsible to constantly strive for «the realization of the political, economic, and cultural unity of the Islamic World.»[67]

In order to preserve their power in Iran, the mullahs have always tried to gain influence in other Muslim countries of the region. The Iran-Iraq war, which on the insistence of Khomeini continued for eight years and resulted in the deaths of over a million Iranians, as well as the mullahs' current domination over parts of Iraq and Lebanon serve as examples of this policy. Such reactionary expansionism, which has occurred at the expense of the unjust shedding of the blood of innocent people accompanied by a horrendous scale of destruction, are contradictory to the teachings of Islam.

Misogyny

Among the other clear and predominant common features of fundamentalists is their misogyny. This is the implementation of inequality and violence against women, depriving them of their basic freedoms and rights, barring them from management and leadership roles in sociopolitical institutions, and considering them as second-class citizens, all of which occur by using Islam as the excuse. But when Islam was introduced, it played a pioneering role in opening the path of liberty and equality for women. For example, from the earliest days, hundreds of women gained prominence by swearing allegiance to the Prophet and assuming responsibilities to assist the Prophet in political, social and military matters.[68]

The Quran highlights equality among all human beings, including women and men. The dynamism of Islam and the Quran annuls all rulings that in one way or another reject gender equality.

Takfir (Excommunication)

Khomeini, Daesh, and other similar entities use Takfir to suppress and eliminate opponents and especially to confront those who oppose the mullahs' Sharia.

Khomeini's religious decree to massacre political prisoners in Iran in 1988 is one of the most important examples of Takfir in modern history. In a handwritten order, Khomeini claimed that sympathizers of the People's Mojahedin Organization of Iran (PMOI/MEK) are not «in any way» committed to Islam and are sentenced to death in various prisons across Iran. On the basis of this order, in the span of a few months, over 30,000 political prisoners, most of whom were supporters of the PMOI, were executed. But, according to the Quran and the traditions of the Prophet, the spirit of Islam is intertwined with tolerance and acceptance of disagreements and differences among human beings, groups, and followers of various faiths and religions. In verse 87 of The Cow, God vociferously reprimands those who ban others, saying that they are pompous and reject one group while killing another.[69]

Dogmatism with respect to secondary issues combined with neglect of humanitarian principles

One of the disgraceful beliefs of all fundamentalists, from which they do not shy away, lies in the attempt to discredit moral, humanitarian and Islamic principles to reach their own petty goals, especially in their quest to preserve power.

They are extremely fastidious, inflexible and dogmatic when it comes to secondary and inconsequential issues. At the same time, when it comes to the fundamental principles and ideals of Islam, they commit heresy and are negligent in accordance with their own interests. In the words of Jesus, they can strain out a gnat and swallow a camel.

Before obtaining power, Khomeini in his most important book entitled «The Islamic State» deemed as permissible mass killings in order to ensure the survival of the state or, as he put it, in order to «uproot many of the corrupt races that are harmful to society.»[70] After he came to power, he also said: «The vali-e faqih (clerical ruler) can prevent prayers, fasting and Haj if he finds such prevention expedient ... and to destroy the house of a believer and secure the divorce of the man's wife.»[71]

And as everyone witnessed, in order to preserve his rule, he continued the devastating Iran-Iraq war for eight years and left a million victims among the Iranian people.

Today, Daesh, which massacres people without a moment's pause, is following the same example and lends no value or credence to humanitarian or moral principles.

By the way, is it not true that monotheistic religions were revealed in order to ensure the compliance of human beings with moral codes and humanitarian principles?

Were the Ten Commandments of Moses or everything that Jesus and Mohammad said not intended to contain the aggressive, greedy and oppressive tendencies of human beings in order to inaugurate a path toward freedom and the realization of individual and social ideals?

So how can fundamentalists give permission to themselves to commit all sorts of brutality and dub it Islam?

It is astonishing that fundamentalists, in all their Shiite and Sunni variants, portray themselves as defenders of Islamic and moral standards. In order to implement unjustified violence, which they falsely describe as «Islamic punishments,» they have amputated many limbs, gouged out eyes and stoned women to death with indescribable barbarity and callousness. While in this age, no one has trampled upon divine and Islamic laws more than this bunch. As the Quran says, «And of men is he whose speech about the life of this world pleases thee, and he calls Allah to witness as to that which is in his heart, yet he is the most violent of adversaries. And when he holds authority, he makes effort in the land to cause mischief in it and destroy tilth and offspring; and Allah loves not mischief.»[72]

Our beliefs

All this is not a mere theoretical treatise for our movement. It is the subject of a difficult struggle, which has continued for the last five decades at a heavy price that includes many lives. The history of the PMOI is a history of persistent theoretical and practical rebellion against the foundations of reactionary religious ideology.

The PMOI is the oldest and largest Muslim organization in the Middle East that opposes extremist interpretations of Islam. The PMOI was founded in 1965. Ever since, it embarked on a theoretical effort to understand the truth of Islam and wipe away the dogmatic and static readings of it. The PMOI succeeded in formulating and promoting in Iranian society the credible views of Islam on freedom, human rights, social justice, gender equality, the rights of ethnic and religious minorities and other matters.

The thinking proffered by PMOI founder Mohammad Hanifnejad marked a revolution in Islamic thought. He said that the true demarcation is not between believers and non-believers of God. The real demarcation line lies between those who suppress and oppress others, and those who are being suppressed and exploited.

This outlook marked a definitive and unyielding gulf between the traditional and static understanding of Islam on the one hand and the true Islam on the other. It marked an indisputable boundary between the PMOI or a democratic Islam and a reactionary Islam.

On this basis, today, we reject sectarianism and religious conflicts. We declare that the struggle is not between Shiites and Sunnis, or Muslims and Christians, or the people and culture of the Middle East against the people and culture of the West.

Yes, there is no war of civilizations. Rather, the main struggle is between tyranny and fundamentalism on the one hand, and democracy, freedom and people who seek freedom and progress on the other.

Other steps taken by the PMOI in the context of the theoretical and ideological struggle against religious reactionary thinking are just as important. In circumstances where traditional culture ruled over a majority in Iranian society, the PMOI, with incredible bravery, stood up to the reactionary mullahs, referenced the Quran[73] and said that a correct understanding of Islam is dependent on one's participation in the struggle to produce social change. And this is something that the reactionary ayatollahs who justify crimes committed by ruling regimes cannot do.

In contrast to the mullahs who view scientific achievements and theories like the evolution of life and society as contradictory to their reactionary understanding of Islam and the Quran, the PMOI sees these theories as conforming and complementary to the ideological and anthropological viewpoints outlined in the Quran and Islam. The PMOI considers the emergence of prophets and prominent religions like Islam as the biggest change inducers for social evolution in history.

These are among the subjects that the Iranian Resistance's Leader Massoud Rajavi taught in the early years after the anti-monarchical revolution. At the time, the French Daily Le Monde wrote, «One of the most important events not to be missed in Tehran is the course on comparative philosophy, taught every Friday afternoon by Mr. Massoud Rajavi. Some 10,000 people present their admission cards to listen for three house to the lectures by the leader of the People's Mojahedin on Sharif University's lawn.» [74]

Moreover, the PMOI embraced the theory of «Quranic dynamism,» which supplies the framework and context for a correct understanding of the Quran. Inspired by Islamic principles, this context affirms the legitimacy of secular legislation while annulling and rejecting fundamentalist Sharia laws whose special role is to enchain social freedoms.

The PMOI, inspired by the principle of free will and choice embedded in Islamic and Quranic teachings, rose up to defend the people's freedom and sovereignty, declaring anything based on tyranny and refusal of the people's free vote as alien to Islam. The

Iranian Resistance's initiative to call for the abolition of the death penalty, a rare example in Islamic countries, was the practical upshot of such an outlook.

In this context, the PMOI rose up against the velayat-e faqih (absolute clerical rule) in Iran. Paying a heavy price, they rejected the mullahs' constitution, which has the velayat-e faqih as its pillar. They also disavowed and renounced the demagoguery of the mullahs, who claimed that they were representatives of God on earth.

The PMOI also launched a drawn out and profound struggle for gender equality. By making reference to the Quran and the traditions of the Prophet and other Islamic pioneers, they showed that denying women their rights and freedoms is contradictory to the true message of Islam. This belief has had a tangible and real impact on the structure of the resistance movement. Women have attained a decisive role in the leadership of this movement as well as in other levels of decision making.

And, ultimately, the PMOI's crucial trailblazing act has been the promotion of the separation of religion and state, which leaves no room for theocracy and religious discrimination. Support for this principle could not have attained the seriousness and impact that it has had if it were not a Muslim movement's initiative. Throughout the Middle East and Muslim countries, this serves as the only example where a Muslim resistance movement has been able to defend the principle of separation of religion and state and open the way for the establishment of democracy.

In defense of this principle, we have risen up against coercive religion and religious coercion. Can this principle be considered as creating limitations or introducing revisions in Islam's fundamental ideas? No, to the contrary, it insists on the true spirit of Islam, which in the words of Massoud Rajavi «takes exception to any justification or legitimacy, including political legitimacy, borne out of coercion and compulsion. ... We profoundly believe that Islam's true blossoming becomes possible when no social or political discrimination, privilege, or coercion is used.»

By the separation of religion and state, do we mean that in a society liberated from dictatorship no individual or group can be active by relying on Islam? No, what we mean is that, just as a resolution adopted by the National Council of Resistance of Iran says, the ballot box reigns supreme and no privilege should be granted or taken away due to belief or lack of belief in a particular religion. This principle also guarantees freedom of religion in the sense that Muslims or followers of other faiths can freely practice their religion without facing any form of inequality whatsoever.

In a document he prepared in 633 in the city of Medina, the Prophet of Islam said: «Jews and Muslims are like one nation or people. (The only difference is that) the Jews follow their religion and the Muslims are committed to their own.»[75]

What we are advocating is to annul and reject tyranny under the veil of religion. This is the conclusion reached from a great historical experience, which foresaw the defeat of religious dictatorship in Iran. Our goal is to overthrow the foundation of sectarianism under the guise of Shiism or Sunnism. Exploiting religion for the pursuit of power must not continue any longer.

Endnotes

1. Sahifeh Noor (Book of Light, a collection of Khomeini's sayings), volumes 19, Chapter 11: "You must tell people about Islam… Why don't you read the Chapter of Repentance to the people?... Why don't you read them the verses on war? You keep reading the verses on compassion. Killing is also a form of mercy because it corrects people. People sometimes don't correct their behavior unless they are burnt, or cut so that the society is rewarded with rectification. Those who are corrupt must be expelled from society."
2. The Bee, verse 125.
3. The Crowds, verse 18.
4. The Cow, verse 111.
5. The Family of Imran, verse 159.
6. The following verses attest to this call:
   The Children of Israel, verse 105.
   The Criterion, verse 5.
   The Confederates, verse 45-48.
   The city of Saba', verse 28.
   The Angels, verse 24.
   The Opening Chapter, verse 8.
   The Cow, verse 119.
7. The Quran, Chapter 33, verse 72: "Indeed, we offered the Trust to the heavens and the earth and the mountains, and they

declined to bear it and feared it; but man [undertook to] bear it. Indeed, he was unjust and ignorant.''

8. The Thunder, verse 11.

9. Nahj-ol Balagha (The Road to Eloquence), letter no. 53.

10. Massoud Rajavi, speech entitled, "Dynamism of the Quran and two diametrically opposed readings of Islam", Eid al-Fitr, 1997.

11. On March 30, 2014, Molavi Abdollah Baji Zehi, prayer leader of Shirabad Mosque of Zahedan, was shot four times in the head when leaving the mosque. On the same day, two Baluchi citizens, 34 and 40, with the surname Shahoozehi were killed by barrage of gunfire of government mercenaries.
On March 31, 2014, Mr. Morad Kahra Zehi, 45, was shot eight times in Zahedan and seriously wounded. On April 1, Mr. Khodad Narouii, 60, was killed by a barrage of gunfire in the city of Bazman, in Iranshahr.

12. As for the regional solution, Maryam Rajavi said in the gathering of Iranians in Paris on June 13, 2015: "Today, western and Arab world's policy makers stress that ISIS and Bashar Assad are two sides of the same coin. I add that the Caliph in Tehran is the godfather of both of them. The fact is that ISIS emerged out of the atrocities perpetrated by Bashar Assad and (former Iraqi Prime Minister Nouri) Maliki on the orders of the clerical regime. I, therefore, call upon western governments to refrain from taking the side of the Tehran regime. In Iraq, do not collaborate with the regime's Islamic Revolutionary Guards Corps (IRGC) and the so-called Shiite militias who are a hundred times more dangerous than the other henchmen. The solution in Iraq is to evict the mullahs' regime forces, to empower the Sunnis, and to arm the Sunni tribes. The solution in Syria is to evict the Iranian regime's forces and to support the people of Syria in overthrowing Assad's dictatorship. The solution in Yemen is to stand up to Tehran, as the Arab coalition has already done. This must be pursued until the regime is uprooted all across the region. Indeed, the solution is to evict the Iranian

regime from the entire region and to topple the Caliph of regression and terrorism in Iran."

13. The Heights, verse 157.
14. The Cow, verse 34.
15. The Man, verse 3.
16. The Sun, verse 8.
17. The Thunder, verse 11.
18. The Family of Imran, verse 64.
19. The Cow, verse 256.
20. The Jonah, verse 20.
21. The Prophet Hud, verse 28.
22. The Road to Eloquence, Letter 53.
23. Ibid.
24. This is a reference to the women, members of the Iranian Resistance, who lead the opposition force and were based at the time in Camp Ashraf, Iraq.
25. The Family of Imran, verse 159.
26. The Heights, verse 157.
27. This gathering was held on June 26, 2010, in the stadium of the city of Taverny, in Val d'Oise, France.
28. The Prophets, verse 107.
29. Islamic Government, page 65, published in Najaf in 1971.
30. In 1944, when he was in his 50s, Khomeini wrote another book called, Kashf-ol Asrar (Discovering the Secrets), but he did not even point to the idea of seizing political power and his maximum demand was for the government to comply with Islam. In this book, he wrote: "We fear a black revolution, a revolution from below (i.e. by the masses)." He also wrote that mullahs like him "never opposed the country's government." And even if "they recognize the government as being despotic, they would never oppose it" and "therefore, the things that set limit to government and velayat are not more than a few. Therefore, fatwas, judgments and interventions in protecting the property of minors and underage do not make any mentions

to the government or the monarchy" and "no jurisprudent has ever said or written in any book that we are kings and monarchy is our right" and "has never opposed or attempted to upset the foundations of government" or "this class has never expressed opposition to the principle of monarchy."

31. Sahifey-e Nour, Collected speeches of Khomeini, Vol. 11.

32. In amending the Constitution of the clerical regime in 1989, they officially inserted the term Velayat Motlaqeh Amr (Absolute Guardianship of Affairs) in principle 57 of the Constitution. It notes, "The ruling branches in the Islamic Republic of Iran are the Legislature, Executive and Judiciary which are administered under the supervision of the Absolute velayat-e faqih, according to the future principles of this law. These forces are independent."

33. Ressalat newspaper, August 15, 1988.

34. Ressalat newspaper, August 20, 1988.

35. Khomeini's letter to Khamenei, January 7, 1988.

36. Ibid.

37. Sahifey-e Nour, Vol. 15: "When Islam is in danger, all of you are obliged to protect Islam by espionage. When protecting the blood of Muslims is an obligation for all, if protecting the life of a Muslim depends on your drinking alcohol, you are obliged to do so. Lie, you are obliged to do so. Islamic laws are for the interests of Muslims, for the interest of Islam. If we see that Islam is in danger, all of us must die to protect it. If we see that the lives of Muslims are in danger, if we see that a bunch of people are conspiring to attack and kill a group of innocents, we are obliged to spy. All of us are obliged to monitor, pay attention and do not allow such a thing happen. Protecting the lives of Muslims is above other things. Protecting Islam is prior even to the lives of Muslims. These are foolish talks coming from these groups that it is not good to spy! Corrupt spying is what is not good. But to protect Islam and to protect the lives of Muslims, it is obligatory. Lying is also an obligation and drinking alcohol is

also an obligation."

38. The Holy Quran, Chapter The Cow, verses 204-205.

39. The Holy Quran, Chapter Sad, verse 72: "When I have fashioned him [in due proportion] and breathed into him of My spirit, fall ye down in obeisance unto him."

40. Narration, verse 5.

41. Hajj-ul-wida, excerpt:

«ايها الناس ان الله قد اذهب عنكم نخوة الجاهلية و تفاخرها بابائها، الا انكم من آدم و آدم من طين، ان العربية ليست باب والد و لكنها لسان ناطق، فمن قصر به عمله لم يبلغ به حسبه، ان الناس من عهد آدم الى يومنا هذا مثل اسنان المشط لا فضلَ لعربي على عجمي و لا للاحمر على الاسود الا بالتقوى. اَلا ان كل مال و مأثرة و دم فى الجاهلية كان تحت قدمي هاتين».

"All mankind is from Adam's generation, an Arab has no superiority over a non-Arab nor a non-Arab has any superiority over an Arab; also a white has no superiority over black nor a black any superiority over white - except by piety and good action. Learn that every Muslim is a brother to every Muslim and that the Muslims constitute one brotherhood. Nothing shall be legitimate to a Muslim which belongs to a fellow Muslim unless it was given freely and willingly. Do not, therefore, do injustice to yourselves."

42. Throughout the Quran, it emphasizes the equality and common responsibility of men and women. In hundreds of cases, they are addressed on an equal footing, including in the Chapter called The Confederates. The Quran addresses men and women without any distinctions. The Confederates, verse 35: "For Muslim men and women,- for believing men and women, for devout men and women, for true men and women, for men and women who are patient and constant, for men and women who humble themselves, for men and women who give in Charity, for men and women who fast [and deny themselves], for men and women who guard their chastity, and for men and women who engage much in Allah's praise,- for them has Allah prepared forgiveness and great reward."

43. The Crowds, verses 17-18.

44. The treaty was signed in the 11th year after the Prophet's emigration.

45. Abdol-Hossein Zarrinkoob, Record of Islam (Karnameh Islam)

46. Mohammad Taghi Mesbah Yazdi, Philosophy of Rights (Falsafeh Hoghough), pp. 75-85. [Mesbah Yazdi died in February 2016].

47. Massoud Rajavi, speech delivered at a National Liberation Army of Iran base camp, Eid-al Fitr, 1997.

48. The Family of Imran, verse 159: "It is part of the Mercy of Allah that thou dost deal gently with them Wert thou severe or harsh-hearted, they would have broken away from about thee: so pass over [Their faults], and ask for [Allah's] forgiveness for them; and consult them in affairs [of moment]. Then, when thou hast taken a decision put thy trust in Allah. For Allah loves those who put their trust [in Him]."

49. The Consultation, verses 36-40: "Whatever ye are given [here] is [but] a convenience of this life: but that which is with Allah is better and more lasting: [it is] for those who believe and put their trust in their Lord:
Those who avoid the greater crimes and shameful deeds, and, when they are angry even then forgive;
Those who hearken to their Lord, and establish regular Prayer; who [conduct] their affairs by mutual Consultation; who spend out of what We bestow on them for Sustenance;
And those who, when an oppressive wrong is inflicted on them, [are not cowed but] help and defend themselves.
The recompense for an injury is an injury equal thereto [in degree]: but if a person forgives and makes reconciliation, his reward is due from Allah: for [Allah] loveth not those who do wrong."

50. المشاوره من السنه والاستبداد من شيمه الانسان

51. In his book, Tanbih-ul Ummah va Tanzih-ul Mellah, Na'ini says: Just as it is slavery and servitude if one obeys despotic rulers and surrenders to the arbitrary will of oppressive Sultans,

surrendering to the arbitrary orders of religious leaders and heads of state which are presented as worship, is considered slavery. Removing the 'evil dynasty' of political and governmental despotism is much easier than uprooting religious tyranny." Religious dictatorship has always protected the evil dynasty of despotism in the name of protecting religion. It has always tried knowingly to confuse falsehood with truth. Religious despotism always denies the importance of a parliamentary and constitutional regime based on the foundations of national rights and responsibility of authorities. Despotic Ulema (clergy) not only ridicule the people's lost freedoms, but brand anti-dictatorial struggle as heresy and heterodoxy. Yes, despotic clergy are hijackers of faith and mislead the Muslim poor. This story narrated from the Prophet, is completely true about them which says: "The harm of this group of clergy for the unaware and uneducated people is more than the harm of the army of Yazid for Imam Hussein (SA)."

Religious despotism is more dangerous than other tyrannical forces because their representatives infiltrate the hearts of people by religion. These clergies are like "worshipers of the world such as Amr-o As, Mohammad-ibn Muslem, Muslem-ibn Mokhled, Moghireh-ibn Sho'beh" who were "considered by the public as companions of the Prophet of Islam" and were thus highly respected and followed by the people. While they were "engaged in duplicity under the name of religion."

In the name of religion, they collaborated with Mo'aviyeh to overcome Ali-ibn Abi-Talib and establish their rule by despotic methods. In fact, religious despotism in Islam was mixed with political despotism at the time of Mo'aviyeh, to counter the truth presented by Imam Ali. Since then, the tradition of political and religious despotism has continued. Unfortunately, it is very difficult and almost impossible to "cure religious despotism." "Malicious clergy, hijackers of the faith and those who mislead the poor" would not be guided to the right path.

In Na'ini's view, this type of clergies have always supported tyranny, from the onset.

The despotic clergy had declared that the constitutional system is against Islam and accused constitutionalists of advocating atheism and heresy. The main issues the clergy had found against Islam were: Freedom, equality of men and women, equality of Muslims and non-Muslims, rule of the majority, legislation, changing the laws, financial fines, punishment of people according to the law not the scholars' decrees, and a parliamentary and representative system replacing the rule of the Velayat.

In addition, the despotic clergy said that constitutional system in Europe that looks so attractive and adorable to some Muslims, actually blocks the clergy's practice of interpreting the Quran, takes away the right of judgement from religious scholars and grants it to normal non-scholar arbiters, and sees government as relying on people not on God. The critical clergy believed that all of the above-said trample upon Islamic laws and instructions. (Mahallati, Al-Le'ali Al-Marbouteh, pp. 20-75)

Contrary to such claims, Na'ini believed in the principle of equality of all people with the ruler in public affairs and in enjoying other privileges. He considered the privileges as the people's unalienable rights. These affairs are part of the certain rights of Muslims and one of the basic principles of democracy which Na'ini supported without any hesitation or doubt.

52. Jahangir Gha'em-Maghami, specialist on Iran's historical documents in the book, "Historical documents of the Iranian Constitutional incidents."

53. Ayatollah Seyyed Mahmoud Taleqani, Friday prayer sermon, Tehran, September 8, 1979.

54. The Table Spread, verse 35: "On that account: We ordained for the Children of Israel that if any one slew a person --unless it be for murder or for spreading mischief in the land -- it would be as if he slew the whole people: And if any one saved a life, it would

be as if he saved the life of the whole people."

55. The Overwhelming Event, verses 21-22.
56. The Thunder, verse 20.
57. The Gathering, verse 9.
58. The Inner Apartments, verse 13.
59. Ijtihad means interpretation of Allegorical verses of the Quran by qualified scholars. This principle requires Islamic scholars and sociologists to develop Islamic methods and rules appropriate to the times.
60. Quran, The Cow, Verse 106
61. Quran, The Bees, verse 101
62. Imam Ali, Nahj-ol Balagha (The Road To Eloquence), Sermon 1
63. Quran, The Overwhelming Event, verses 21 and 22
64. Tabari, Tabari History, volume 3, published in Beirut
65. Imam Ali, Nahj-ol Balagha (The Road To Eloquence), letter no. 53
66. Quran, The Examined One, verses 8 and 9: «Allah forbids you not respecting those who fight you not for religion, nor drive you forth from your homes, that you show them kindness and deal with them justly. Surely Allah loves the doers of justice. Allah forbids you only respecting those who fight you for religion, and drive you forth from your homes and help (others) in your expulsion, that you make friends of them; and whoever makes friends of them, these are the wrongdoers.»
67. Constitution of the Islamic Republic of Iran, Article 11.
68. Ibn Saad, al-Tabaghat al-Kobra, Volume 7
69. Also in The Women, verse 94: «O you who believe, when you go forth (to fight) in Allah's way, make investigation, and say not to anyone who offers you salutation, Thou art not a believer, seeking the good of this world's life. But with Allah there are abundant gains. You too were such before, then Allah conferred a benefit on you; so make investigation. Surely Allah is ever Aware of what you do.»
70. Ruhollah Khomeini, Islamic State, 1971.

71. State-run daily Ressalat, August 20, 1988.
72. Quran, The Cow, verses 204 and 205.
73. Quran, The Spider, verse 69: «And those who strive hard for Us, We shall certainly guide them in Our ways. And Allah is surely with the doers of good.»
74. Le Mode, March 1, 1980
75. Ibn Hisham, As-Sirah, Volume 1, P. 334.